Advance praise for
Don't Hit My Mommy!

"Alicia Lieberman and Patricia Van Horn have given a crucial 'voice' to young children traumatized by exposure to domestic violence. They describe in detail a creative and effective therapeutic strategy to help these children and their victimized parents. Their sensitive and masterful approach to treatment through child–parent psychotherapy will help not only the child victims, but also their vulnerable families."

    – **Joy D. Osofsky**, PhD, Professor of Pediatrics, Psychiatry, & Public Health, Director, Harris Center for Infant Mental Health, Louisiana State University Health Sciences Center

"In this sure-to-be seminal volume, Alicia Lieberman and Patricia Van Horn draw upon their extensive knowledge of early child development and their years of experience in providing child–parent psychotherapy to high-risk children and families. In so doing, they demystify this powerful psychotherapeutic modality, which is a product of the dynamic interplay among research on the effects of intrafamilial violence on young children, theoretical perspectives that integrate attachment and psychodynamic theories, and clinical case material. Don't Hit My Mommy! will be invaluable to therapists of all persuasions who work with young children. Most importantly, it will increase the availability of child–parent psychotherapy to families who otherwise might not have access to this evidence-based form of treatment."

    – **Dante Cicchetti**, PhD, Director, Mt. Hope Family Center, University of Rochester

"DON'T HIT MY MOMMY!"

A Manual for Child–Parent Psychotherapy With Young Witnesses of Family Violence

"DON'T HIT MY MOMMY!"

A Manual for Child–Parent Psychotherapy With Young Witnesses of Family Violence

Alicia F. Lieberman and Patricia Van Horn

ZERO
TO
THREE®

National Center for Infants,
Toddlers, and Families

Washington, D.C.

ZERO TO THREE
National Center for Infants,
Toddlers, and Families

Published by
ZERO TO THREE
1255 23rd St., NW, Ste. 350
Washington, DC 20037
(202) 638-1144
Toll-free orders (800) 899-4301
Fax: (202) 638-0851
Web: http://www.zerotothree.org

The mission of the ZERO TO THREE Press is to publish authoritative research, practical resources, and new ideas for those who work with and care about infants, toddlers, and their families. Books are selected for publication by an independent Editorial Board.

The views contained in this book are those of the authors and do not necessarily reflect those of ZERO TO THREE: National Center for Infants, Toddlers and Families, Inc.

Cover design: Jennifer Paul
Text design: Design Consultants, Inc.

Library of Congress Cataloging-in-Publication Data

Lieberman, Alicia F.
  Don't hit my mommy! : a manual for child-parent psychotherapy with young witnesses of family violence / Alicia F. Lieberman and Patricia Van Horn.– 1st ed.
     p. cm.
  Includes bibliographical references.
  ISBN 0-943657-84-9; 978-0-943657-84-4
  1. Children of abused wives–Mental health. 2. Victims of family violence–Mental health. 3. Abused children–Mental health. 4. Child psychotherapy–Parent participation. 5. Psychic trauma in children–Treatment. 6. Infants–Mental health. 7. Toddlers–Mental health. 8. Preschool children–Mental health. I. Van Horn, Patricia. II. Title.
  RJ507.F35L54 2004
  616.85'8220651–dc22

                           2004017825

10   9   8   7   6

Suggested citation:
Lieberman, A. F., & Van Horn, P. (2005). *Don't hit my mommy!: A manual for child–parent psychotherapy for young witnesses of family violence.* Washington, D.C.: ZERO TO THREE Press.

To Selma Fraiberg,

who understood the magic of the early years

TABLE OF CONTENTS

TABLE OF CONTENTS CONTINUED

ACKNOWLEDGMENTS

THIS MANUAL IS THE PRODUCT OF MANY YEARS of providing child–parent psychotherapy to young children and their parents as they struggle to change the violence and hopelessness of their family bonds and find more security, pleasure, and love within themselves and in each other. We thank the countless parents who trust us as allies in their efforts, allowing us into the privacy of their closest relationships. We are particularly grateful to the children, who are our persistent teachers in showing us what they need until we finally understand and are able to respond.

The development of this manual involved an active collaborative process. Drafts of the work were discussed monthly over the course of 2 years during our case review at the Child Trauma Research Project (CTRP), and the feedback from our colleagues and students spurred us toward greater specificity in the description of intervention strategies. The clinical examples, derived from their detailed narrative session notes, owe much to their talent and creativity. Our current program faculty—Nancy Compton, Chandra Ghosh Ippen, Laura Castro, and Laura Mayorga—has been steadfast in providing us with a sturdy secure base where the challenges of treating families experiencing violence can be shared as we search together for a helpful course of action and where the joys of progress can be jointly celebrated. Donna Davidovitz, Robin Silverman, Eddie Walden, and Maria Augusta Torres participated in shaping our direction during the earlier years of the program, and their contributions continue to be valued.

We learn much from the interns and postdoctoral fellows who spend 1, 2, or 3 years with us, bringing their unique outlooks and skills. There are now more than 50 graduates of the program, and the sheer number precludes our naming them individually. They know, however, that they constitute our extended family and continue to be remembered and appreciated for their commitment to the children, the families, and the work.

Being part of the University of California–San Francisco (UCSF) and San Francisco General Hospital is an integral part of our programmatic and professional identities. We could not have written this manual without the inspiration and support of Robert L. Okin, Chief of the Department of Psychiatry at San Francisco General Hospital. His invitation to launch the CTRP in 1996 gave us the impetus to develop and evaluate evidence-based approaches to the treatment of traumatic stress in young children. His unwavering commitment to the underserved has transformed the landscape of mental health services in San Francisco, and we are among the many beneficiaries of his vision. Craig Van Dyke, Chair of the UCSF Department of Psychiatry, is an exemplary leader in promoting the individual academic pursuits of the faculty while fostering a spirit of collaboration within a large and diverse department.

We are very grateful to our present and past funders for providing both financial support and opportunities for constructive dialogue. The cornerstone of the CTRP consists of an agreement between the San Francisco General Hospital, the Department of Public Health, and the Department of Human Services (DHS). We thank Sai-Ling Chan-Sew as well as DHS managers, supervisors, and child welfare workers for many years of productive partnership on behalf of traumatized young children that provide the groundwork for this manual. The National Institute of Mental Health supported our pilot randomized trial of manual-guided child–parent psychotherapy through an R21 Exploratory/Development grant. Our scientific review administrator, Victoria Levin, is legendary among grantees for integrating extraordinary knowledge with unmatched selflessness in sharing it.

This institutional support has been buttressed by the generosity of private foundations and individual donors. Irving Harris was quick to recognize both the urgency and the obstacles involved in addressing the effects of trauma in the early years, and his ongoing contribution underwrites the infrastructure and training components of our program. The Coydog Foundation and William Harris are enabling us to explore new angles in the interface between trauma and attachment through the beneficial effect of loving experiences in guiding the restoration of healthy bonds. The Miriam and Peter Haas Fund enabled us to develop productive collaborations with Child Protective Services and with the courts, and Cheryl Polk shared her talent and expertise in program development. The A. L. Mailman Foundation and the Nathan Cummings Foundation supported the inclusion in the manual of intervention strategies developed for the first 2 years of life. The Pinewood Foundation, the Francis S. North Foundation, and the George Sarlo Foundation made possible the development of intervention strategies geared specifically to the experiences of immigrant and minority families facing violence. Gifts from Jonathan and Kathleen Altman, from Aubrey and Beverly Metcalf, and from the Isabel Allende Foundation allow us to respond to unanticipated needs. Our sense of indebtedness to all of them gives substance to Felix Frankfurter's observation that "gratitude is one of the least articulate of emotions, especially when it is deep."

The manual profited immensely from the input of cherished colleagues and friends. Dante Cicchetti, Scott Henggeler, Arietta Slade, and Sheree Toth reviewed an early draft and were generous with their clinical insights and editorial skills. Elizabeth Power contributed her expertise with manual development. Our participation in the National Child Traumatic Stress Network (NCTSN) of the Substance Abuse and Mental Health Services Administration (SAMHSA) enabled us to establish the Early Trauma Treatment Network as a collaborative among our program and three groundbreaking programs working with young children exposed to interpersonal violence at Boston Medical Center, Louisiana State University Health Science Center, and Tulane University. We thank their directors and our partners in this collaborative, Betsy McAlister Groves, Joy Osofsky, Julie Larrieu, and Charles Zeanah for their thoroughness and zeal in implementing the manual in their training and treatment protocols and for sharing their extensive experience and valuable clinical insights with us. Our understanding of traumatic stress was greatly enhanced through the seminal work of other members of the NCTSN, including Robert Pynoos, Bessel van der Kolk, Judy Cohen, and Steven Marans. Our deep thanks for their readiness to make their knowledge available to us. We have also learned a great deal from local collaborators. Our colleagues at the San Francisco Unified Family Court, the Safe Start Initiative, and in the domestic violence advocacy community all gave us their valuable perspectives on the families that we serve. Their contributions greatly enriched our work.

Work is done best when supported by a sustaining home life. We thank our partners, David Richman and Verlene Perry, for many things: their love, their unfaltering support during this project and, perhaps above all, for their forbearance during the long hours we spent in bringing it to fruition.

San Francisco, July 2003

INTRODUCTION

"My daddy makes my mommy cry, and my mommy makes me cry, and that's how it works." Sandra, 3 years old.

"Even a fist was once an open palm with fingers." Yehuda Amichai.

THE ORIGINS OF AN AGGRESSIVE STANCE toward other people can be traced to the earliest years of childhood, to experiences of helplessness and pain that instill in the child a conviction that being on the offensive is the best defense. Witnessing violence and being the victim of violence shatter the child's confidence that his well-being matters and that adults will take care of him. Little Sandra, at age 3, displayed a philosopher's analytical skills when she concluded, on the basis of her family experience, that making somebody cry is the way of the world. At the same time, she strenuously protested this state of affairs when she screamed: "Don't hit my mommy!" in a frantic but futile effort to protect her mother by stopping her father's violence. Millions of children who are exposed to family violence share Sandra's internal dilemma of yearning for safety while at the same time learning that the people she loves make each other cry. The question she left unspoken is: Will Sandra also make someone cry someday? Will she become the next link in the crying chain? Or is it possible to reach her before her hand becomes a fist, while it is still "an open palm with fingers?"

This manual is designed to provide treatment guidelines to address the behavioral and mental health problems of infants, toddlers, and preschoolers whose most intimate relationships are disrupted by the experience of violence.

Although the primary focus is on children who have witnessed domestic violence, the intervention strategies described in the manual apply to many forms of child maltreatment as well. It is now widely accepted that witnessing or experiencing acts of severe interpersonal violence interferes with the mastery of age-appropriate developmental milestones and leaves children at significant risk for conduct disorder, posttraumatic stress disorder, anxiety, and depression (Margolin, 1998; Osofsky & Scheeringa, 1997; Pynoos, 1993; Rossman, Hughes, & Rosenberg, 2000). In spite of extensive data documenting these risks, and in spite of evidence that preschoolers may be at greater risk than older children (Fantuzzo, Brouch, Beriama, & Atkins, 1997), there is a dearth of intervention strategies designed to alleviate the effects of exposure to violence in the first 5 years of life. This manual has the purpose of providing practitioners from a variety of disciplines with an understanding of the impact of violence and with concrete intervention strategies to address the consequences of this experience for young children.

The manual is divided into four sections. Section I describes the theoretical premises that guide our treatment model, provides an overview of child–parent psychotherapy, and explains how this form of treatment is used with infants, toddlers, and preschool children who have witnessed potentially traumatizing levels of domestic violence. Section II specifies the main domains of intervention and provides itemized descriptions of therapeutic strategies that are unique and essential to child–parent psychotherapy. Section III describes the procedures recommended when the intervention needs to include case management, particularly contacts with the legal system and with Child Protective Services. Section IV provides a list of items that are essential but not unique to child–parent psychotherapy, as well as a list of items that are incompatible with our treatment model, as recommended by Waltz, Addis, Koerner, and Jacobson (1993).

Although we describe specific therapeutic strategies and provide illustrative examples, this manual does not prescribe a step-by-step treatment approach. Development in the first years of life is not linear, and young children's profound individual differences in cognitive, social, and emotional maturation are accompanied by unexpected discontinuities, accelerations, and lapses in the unfolding of the child's developmental timetable. Moreover, parents who are involved in family violence present a broad range of psychological vulnerabilities as well as strengths both as individuals and as caregivers. Child–parent psychotherapy advocates the flexible tailoring of therapeutic interventions to the specific aspects of the child–parent relationship that interfere with the child's healthy development, while supporting the growth-promoting aspects of the relationship. Treatment is informed by the clinician's knowledge of early childhood development, child and adult psychopathology, intersubjective processes, and cultural–ecological factors in the sociology and psychology of violence-related trauma.

We believe that, at its best, therapeutic intervention is co-created by the clinician and the recipient(s) of the treatment, which in child–parent psychotherapy comprise at the very least the child and one parent and may include, depending on the clinical need, both parents and perhaps siblings as well. For this reason, we offer alternative strategies for addressing common therapeutic quandaries, with the knowledge that each clinician's creativity, individual style, and sense of timing will guide and enrich their use.

SECTION I

A RELATIONSHIP-BASED TREATMENT MODEL

CHILD–PARENT PSYCHOTHERAPY IS BASED on five major conceptual premises that highlight the importance of relationships in early mental health. We describe these premises here:

1. The attachment system is the main organizer of children's responses to danger and safety in the first 5 years of life (Ainsworth, 1969; Ainsworth, Blehar, Waters, & Wall, 1978; Bowlby, 1969/1982). From the perspective of attachment theory, witnessing domestic violence and enduring maltreatment damage the child's developmentally appropriate expectation that the parents will be reliably available as protectors. In fact, parents themselves become the sources of danger rather than the ones who protect the child from it. The child learns that the people dearest to him are also the ones who can cause the greatest hurt. The child's senses of self and of trust in others become permeated with fear, anger, mistrust, and hypervigilance, responses that are in conflict with age-appropriate strivings for closeness and safety with the parents (Lieberman & Van Horn, 1998; Main & Hesse, 1990; Pynoos, Steinberg, & Piacentini, 1999).

. These responses are particularly notable in the period from birth to preschool because during this developmental stage children learn primarily from observing and imitating the behavior of cherished adults (Kagan, 1981). Children who observe and imitate aggression from an early age are more likely to become aggressive adolescents and adults and to use aggression as a way of coping with stress in intimate relationships (Kalmuss, 1984). Child–parent psychotherapy has the goal of helping children modulate negative emotions, express feelings in socially acceptable ways, and learn age-appropriate ways of recognizing and respecting the parent's motivations and feelings.

2. Emotional and behavioral problems in infancy and early childhood need to be addressed in the context of the child's primary attachment relationships (Fraiberg, 1980; Lieberman, Silverman, & Pawl, 2000; Lieberman & Zeanah, 1995). The young child's sense of self evolves in the context of relationships with the primary caregivers, and enhancing the emotional quality of those relationships is the most effective vehicle for promoting the child's healthy development. Child–parent psychotherapy strives to create a safer and more protective caregiving environment by encouraging loving, development-promoting interactions and appropriate discipline, and decreasing episodes of aggression and emotional withdrawal in the parent's relationship with the child. This goal is pursued by helping the parent and the child become more accurately attuned and more appropriately responsive to the needs, feelings, and motivations of the other.

3. Risk factors in the first 5 years of life, including disorders of attachment, operate in the context of the transactions between the child and his or her social ecology, including the family, neighborhood, community, and larger society (Cicchetti & Lynch, 1993). The child's parents or surrogate attachment figures may live in circumstances that tax their resources and may be beyond their control, such as poverty; discrimination; low education; unemployment; violent neighborhoods; inadequate housing, transportation, and health services; substance abuse; or mental health problems. Such circumstances affect the child's development both directly, through the negative conditions they create, and indirectly, by impairing the parent's capacity to provide adequate care.

Violence in the home is often multidetermined by a variety of risk factors. Faced with these stressors, parents are often unable to support their children's development unless the intervention includes a concerted effort to improve their own circumstances and well-being (Fraiberg, 1980; Henggeler, Schoenwald, Borduin, Rowland, & Cunningham, 1998). Child–parent psychotherapy has the goal of improving the parent's psychological functioning and parenting competence by offering the therapeutic relationship as a source of emotional support, psychological guidance in self-reflection, and active assistance with problems of living.

4. Interpersonal violence must be recognized as a traumatic stressor that has specific pathogenic repercussions on those who witness it as well as on those who experience it (Pynoos et al., 1999). Moreover, different sources of violence tend to coexist. For example, children who witness domestic violence are much more likely to also be physically abused (Osofsky, 2004). Children who are maltreated or who witness domestic violence can become overwhelmed by intense multisensory stimulation, including physical pain, terrifying visual images, loud screaming, crashing objects, the smell of gunpowder or blood, and frantic movement. Domestic violence and maltreatment often consist of multiple episodes that occur unpredictably over an extended time span, so that the child is confronted with many compounded images and may be unable to create a coherent narrative of the frightening events. This is particularly the case if the young child is at different developmental stages when the different episodes of violence took place—ranging, for example, from the preverbal period to the toddler or preschool years.

Traumatic reminders may affect the quality of the child–parent relationship by triggering traumatic stress responses that are misconstrued by the recipient because they are disconnected from their traumatic origins. Child–parent psychotherapy advocates the use of a dual attachment lens and trauma lens. This dual lens enables the clinician to attend to the effect of trauma on the child–parent relationship and to enhance the relationship as a protective mechanism that can help the child cope more effectively with the trauma.

5. The therapeutic relationship is a necessary mutative factor in treatment. As Sameroff and Emde (1989) pointed out, relationships affect relationships. As a result, the clinician's efforts to bring about positive change in the parent–child relationship can succeed only if the clinician's interactions with the parent and the child are based on sensitivity, empathy, and respect for their experience. By reflecting together on the child's and the parent's motivations, feelings, and needs, the clinician and the parent develop a collaborative agenda in which they work together toward jointly held intervention goals.

The collaborative agenda may be explicitly articulated or implicitly shared, depending on the parent's and child's communication styles, but it must reflect an agreement to work toward alleviating areas of difficulty in the parent–child interaction; increasing areas of harmony, competence, and well-being; and decreasing areas of conflict and stress. The parent's cultural values, influenced by race, ethnicity, and socioeconomic circumstances, must be incorporated in the intervention as essential components in building a therapeutic alliance. Throughout this manual, references are made to the role of cultural factors in shaping specific intervention strategies.

Overview of Child–Parent Psychotherapy

Child–parent psychotherapy is a relationship-based form of intervention that focuses on the child–parent interaction and on each partner's perceptions of the other. Goals include increasing the parent's and child's age-appropriate capacity to be emotionally attuned to each other's motivations and needs, and changing mutually reinforcing negative interactional patterns. The theoretical target of child–parent psychotherapy is the web of jointly constructed meanings in the child–parent relationship, which emerge from each partner's mental representations of themselves and of each other (Lieberman et al., 2000). In this sense, the intervention targets the parent's and child's inaccurate and maladaptive mental representations of each other, and fosters the motivation to understand and respect the internal world of the other.

<u>Assessment.</u> The assessment process may vary depending on the characteristics of different programs, and it may incorporate structured research instruments or a clinically guided unstructured format. Regardless of its specific format, an adequate assessment must incorporate the following indispensable components (ZERO TO THREE, 1994).

1. Observation of the child in interaction with the primary caregiver(s);

2. Observation of the child in interaction with the assessor;

3. Observation of the child in different conditions (for example, on at least two different occasions; in different ecologically valid settings, such as home and the child-care setting; and/or in different circumstances, such as during free play and structured tasks);

4. Developmental history of the child, including presenting symptoms;

5. Parental description of the child and of the family situation;

6. Evaluation of the parent's psychological functioning and history;

7. Assessment of the family's cultural background, socioeconomic circumstances, and the implications of these factors for the family's child-rearing values and practices.

<u>Treatment.</u> Child–parent psychotherapy uses behavior-based strategies, play, and verbal interpretation as agents of therapeutic change. For young children, action often carries more meaning than words, and showing by example or through play may be the most effective way of teaching. Words and actions must be integrated in the effort to bring meaning to difficult moments and to change damaging patterns of response.

Child–parent psychotherapy represents an integration of psychoanalysis and attachment theory (Ainsworth et al., 1978; Bowlby, 1969/1982), and includes behavior-based techniques derived from developmental theory, cognitive-behavior approaches, and social learning theory, particularly as it relates to how coercive parenting is linked to aggressive and defiant child behavior (Patterson, 1982; Reid & Eddy, 1997; Webster-Stratton, 1996). The intervention supports and reinforces perceptions, attitudes, and behaviors that convey positive affect, age-appropriate assertion or discipline, reciprocal play, joint exploration of the world, and constructive conflict resolution. It targets for change punitive parenting practices and unmodulated and dysregulated parental and child behaviors, particularly symptoms of violence-related trauma, that include externalizing problems such as aggression, defiance, noncompliance, recklessness, and excessive tantrums, and internalizing problems such as multiple fears, inconsolability, separation anxiety, difficulties sleeping, and social and emotional withdrawal (Lieberman, 2004).

Child–parent psychotherapy is an extension of infant–parent psychotherapy, a form of intervention developed to address mental health problems in children from birth to age 3 (Fraiberg, 1980; Lieberman, 1991; Lieberman & Pawl, 1993; Lieberman, Silverman, & Pawl, 2000). Child–parent psychotherapy differs from infant–parent psychotherapy in two main respects. First, it extends the appropriate age range to the child's first 6 years of life. Second, as the child's sense of autonomous agency increases with age, it emphasizes the child's centrality as an active partner in the intervention by making play and the child–parent interaction the foci of the sessions, with a concomitantly lesser emphasis on the parents' narrative of their life's histories (i. e., linking the parents' childhood conflicts to their current parenting difficulties). Both methods have much in common, including their use of the same therapeutic modalities and their reliance on a thorough assessment of parent and child, individually and in interaction with each other, as the basis for an initial formulation of intervention needs.

Although the intervention focuses on family processes and most specifically on the child–parent interaction, every effort is made to tailor these strategies to the family's cultural values and socioeconomic and educational circumstances. For this reason, the model incorporates active assistance with the family's problems of living as a basic ingredient in establishing a collaborative stance with the family. Parents who are immersed in family turmoil, which may include cultural dislocation and socioeconomic hardship, are seldom able to remain emotionally attuned to their children's needs. In fact, they may perceive their children's bids for attention as one more source of strain on their depleted personal resources. In these circumstances, concrete assistance with problems of living is often an essential step in enlisting the parent's willingness to participate in the intervention because it conveys the clinician's ability and willingness to incorporate the parent's perspective into the work.

Child–Parent Psychotherapy in the Treatment of Violence-Related Trauma

Child–parent psychotherapy can be used in any situation in which the relationship between a young child and the parent is negatively affected by the family's difficult circumstances, including parental depression or other mental illness, bereavement, or chronic stress; child constitutional or developmental characteristics that interfere with the formation of a secure and growth promoting attachment; and "poorness of fit" (Chess & Thomas, 1984) in the temperamental styles of parent and child. Each set of factors calls for individually tailored interventions. This manual is designed specifically for situations in which the child–parent relationship and the child's mental health and developmental momentum are damaged by the experience of violence.

Developmental Considerations

Psychotherapy should consider development as a process that encompasses the entire life span. Child–parent psychotherapy focuses on developmental issues as these pertain both to the child and to the parent.

<u>Child development.</u> Infants, toddlers, and preschool children are in a period of rapid developmental change, and their responses to witnessing domestic violence are influenced by their developmental stage (Marans & Adelman, 1997; Osofsky, 1995; Pynoos & Eth, 1985).

During the first year of life, infants cannot express their feelings using language. Instead, they respond with sensorimotor disorganization and disruption of biological rhythms, in the forms, for example, of intense and prolonged crying; unresponsiveness to soothing; movement problems such as flailing, muscular rigidity, restlessness, and agitation; eating disorders such as lack of appetite or excessive eating; sleeping disorders such as difficulty falling asleep, frequent night wakings, and night terrors; and elimination problems such as constipation and diarrhea without apparent organic causes. Numbing of affect may be manifested in the form of sadness, a subdued demeanor, and unresponsiveness to age-appropriate stimulation (Drell, Siegel, & Gaensbauer, 1993).

Toddlers and preschoolers, who can use autonomous mobility, engage in fight-or-flight mechanisms in response to the perception of danger. These mechanisms may involve recklessness and accident proneness, inhibition of exploration, and precocious competence in self-care—patterns that can be seen as distortions of the normative pattern of secure base behavior that is characteristic of the second and third years of life (Lieberman & Zeanah, 1995).

In comparison to infants, toddlers and preschool children make increasing use of language and symbolic play, and they engage in active efforts to understand causality and how the world operates. They often misattribute the reason for frightening events, blaming themselves when parents are angry or when fights erupt between the adults. The internal conflicts resulting from self-blame and from feeling torn between fear of the parents and longing to be close to them are often manifested in externalizing problems such as aggression, defiance, and noncompliance, and in internalizing problems such as excessive fearfulness and withdrawal. These are manifestations of the biologically based "fight-or-flight" response that characterizes an organism's response to danger (Cannon, 1932). Children also may engage in precociously competent and self-protective behaviors when they cannot rely on their parents to feel safe (Lieberman & Zeanah, 1995).

Parental development. Development is an ongoing process that continues throughout one's lifetime. Becoming a parent ushers in an adult developmental stage that offers new opportunities for reworking long-standing maladaptive patterns and finding more satisfying ways of relating to oneself and others (Benedek, 1959). At the same time, the daily demands of being a parent can constitute a relentless challenge to the adult's identity by testing his or her nurturing capacity and sense of personal competence.

Domestic violence represents a formidable risk factor to the healthy development of the capacity to parent. Under the best of circumstances, being a parent is an emotionally demanding task. The ordinary stresses of life, compounded by lack of knowledge about an infant's or toddler's capacity for compliance and self-control, can lead parents to react harshly when children behave in ways that are annoying or burdensome.

Parents who are prone to violence and/or the victims of violence are even more ill-equipped to respond to challenging or unmodulated child behaviors because they themselves have difficulty regulating strong emotion and because they are often anxious, depressed, or suffering from posttraumatic stress disorder. The parents may tend to misperceive their child's behavior as indications that the child is intrinsically "bad," disrespectful, or unloving (Lieberman, 1999); they may see their children's age-appropriate behavior as harmful or dangerous, based on their own trauma-based expectations that the world and people in it are dangerous (Pynoos, Steingberg, & Goenjian, 1996).

Even parents who are usually able to remain emotionally attuned to their children in spite of their personal difficulties may find themselves at a loss in knowing how to respond when their children engage in challenging behaviors. They may react with helpless efforts to placate the child or with impulsive punishment. These responses confirm the child's sense, derived from witnessing domestic violence, that the parent cannot provide a sense of safety and protection. As a result, the parent's responses may unwittingly exacerbate the child's sense of helplessness, anger, and fear. Child–parent psychotherapy is designed to help both parent and child understand and modulate their responses to traumatic reminders, to help them find ways to calm and soothe themselves when faced with upsetting feelings, to restore their trust in one another, and to address these misattunements between the parent and the child.

The Psychological Sequelae of Violence

Violence can be traumatizing, particularly when it is long-lasting and when it occurs in the context of intimate relationships, where safety and protection are preconditions for a sense of personal integrity. Even if its impact is not manifested in a diagnosable psychiatric condition, violence among family members routinely results in alterations of self-perception, affect regulation, relationships with others, and systems of meaning (Herman, 1992; Horowitz & O'Brien, 1986; van der Kolk, 1996). Each of these disturbances has damaging repercussions on the adult's capacity to parent and on the quality of the parent–child relationship.

In infants, toddlers, and preschool children, the experience of violence leads to a disruption of normative developmental processes. As van der Kolk (1987) noted, "the earliest and possibly most damaging psychological trauma is the loss of a secure base" (p. 32). The empirical literature supports this insight, with findings that young children exposed to violence have high levels of internalizing and externalizing problems that include affect dysregulation, difficulty establishing relationships, play reenactment of the traumatic experience, sleep disturbances, bouts of intense fear and uncontrolled crying, regression in developmental achievements, aggression, and noncompliance (Davidson, 1978; Eth & Pynoos, 1985; Gaensbauer, 1994; Parson, 1995; Pruett, 1979; Pynoos & Nader, 1988; Terr, 1981).

These behavior problems do not exist in an individual vacuum: they reflect not only the impact of trauma on the child, but also the stresses of the parent–child relationship in a family environment marked by conflict and strife. These child behaviors are likely to be early expressions of often-described responses to trauma: avoidance of reminders of the traumatic event, emotional numbing, hyperarousal, and intrusive recollections of the trauma (American Psychiatric Association, 1994; Herman, 1992; Scheeringa & Gaensbauer, 2000; van der Kolk, 1987).

In infancy and early childhood, a diagnosis of traumatic stress disorder is made when the child experiences or witnesses an event that involves actual or threatened death or serious injury to the child or others, or a threat to the physical or psychological integrity of the child or others (ZERO TO THREE, 1994). The following manifestations are considered criteria for the disorder:

how do I know it is traumatic stress disorder

1. Reexperiencing of the traumatic event through posttraumatic play, recurrent recollections of the event outside of play, repeated nightmares, distress at exposure to reminders of the trauma, and/or episodes with objective features of a flashback or dissociation.

2. Numbing of responsiveness or interference with developmental momentum, as expressed through increased social withdrawal, restricted range of affect, temporary loss of previously acquired developmental skills, and/or decrease or constriction of play.

3. Increased arousal, as manifested through night terrors, difficulty going to sleep, repeated night wakings, attentional difficulties, hypervigilance, and exaggerated startle responses.

4. Symptoms that were not present before the traumatic event, such as aggression toward peers, adults, or animals; separation anxiety; fear of toileting alone; fear of the dark or other new fears; somatic symptoms; motor reenactments; and/or precociously sexualized behavior.

The critical link between the stress experienced as the result of a traumatic situation and the child's personality development is the formation of trauma-related expectations that shape the biology of the developing child and are expressed through perceptions, feelings, thoughts, and behavior (Pynoos, Steinberg, & Goenjian, 1996). These traumatic expectations alter the developmental trajectory of the child. The level of disturbance is determined by a complex interaction between the child's constitutional characteristics and previous experience, the objective and subjective features of the traumatic experience(s), subsequent reminders of the experience, comorbid conditions, secondary stresses, and environmental supports before, during, and after the traumatic experience (Pynoos, Steinberg, & Wraith, 1995). When the trauma consists of family violence, an extra layer of complexity is added as the child's traumatic expectations interact with the expectations of the parent traumatized by violence.

Looking through the lens of attachment, we see that a child frightened by family violence would naturally seek proximity to a loved and trusted parent, yearning for protection, soothing, and restoration to a state of calm. Through that lens we also see the parent reciprocating, offering care and comfort to a distressed child. When we view the same parent and child through the lens of trauma, however, we see that traumatic expectations and traumatic reminders have distorted their drive toward attachment. The parent and child become frightening reminders of the trauma for one another, and neither is any longer able to experience the parent as a trustworthy source of protection and calm. It is in this trauma-distorted attachment that the child–parent psychotherapist locates the focus of intervention.

Goals and Mechanisms of Treatment in Recovery From Traumatic Experiences

A prerequisite for the treatment of traumatic responses, both for children and adults, is the establishment of a safe environment, both in real life and in the therapeutic setting. This goal can be particularly challenging when the trauma consists of overwhelming exposure to violence that can be recur unpredictably in the family or in the neighborhood. Battered women may be unable to appraise signals of danger realistically because of their own traumatization, leaving them and their children vulnerable to repetition of traumatic experiences. The therapist needs to focus on developing and mobilizing the parent's capacity for self-protection and protection of the child as a cornerstone of the treatment.

what the violence did

Recognition of the traumatic impact of violence is also a prerequisite to the recovery process. Parents tend to underestimate both the extent to which their children were witnesses to the violence and the damaging impact of the violence on the child (Peled, 2000). Child–parent psychotherapy enables the child and the parent to overcome the taboo against speaking about the violence. The clinician acts as a safe mediator between the parent and the child, both of whom are often unable or reluctant to name the violence for fear that acknowledging it will trigger overwhelming feelings of guilt, shame, blame, and loss.

Different approaches to the treatment of trauma, for children as well as adults, share many commonalities in their goals and the mechanisms proposed to achieve them (Marmar, Foy, Kagan, & Pynoos, 1993). The common features target the main symptoms of traumatic response, and are described here.

1. *Encouraging a return to normal development, adaptive coping, and engagement with present activities and future goals.* This is the overarching goal of treatment, both for children and for adults. A central compo-

nent of the intervention is a focus on the continuity of daily living. The child–parent psychotherapist provides support for developmentally appropriate achievements and for daring to try new and adaptive ways of functioning.

2. *Fostering an increased capacity to respond realistically to threat.* Promoting safety is based on the ability to evaluate whether a situation may involve danger. Traumatized children and adults are often impaired in their ability to appraise and respond to cues of danger. They may either minimize or exaggerate danger, and sometimes do both, overreacting to minor stimuli and overlooking serious threats. In children, this tendency is manifested in an alternation of recklessness and accident proneness. On one hand, they may react aggressively to perceived slights, such as a toy being taken away. On the other hand, they might rush into dangerous situations, such as darting across the street or approaching a stranger. The treatment focuses on developing more accurate perceptions of danger and appropriate responses to it.

3. *Maintaining regular levels of affective arousal.* Traumatic events impair the ability to regulate emotion. This impairment creates a "biopsychosocial trap" because neurophysiological disruptions in the regulation of arousal affect other self-regulatory healing mechanisms. For example, numbing, avoidance, and hyperarousal may interfere with the spontaneous extinction of learned conditioning and with the ability to rely on the help of others as a way of restoring a sense of safety (Shalev, 2000). Children appear to be especially prone to sleep disturbances after trauma, including somnambulism, vocalization, motor restlessness, and night terrors (Pynoos, 1990). Sleeplessness can make children more prone to overreact and respond to mild aversive events with anger and aggression. These changes in physiological reactivity are a behavioral analogue of traumatic expectations (Pynoos et al., 1996).

4. *Reestablishing trust in bodily sensations.* The body is the primary stage where affects are experienced and where the memory of the trauma lives on. As a result, the body itself, by "keeping the score" (van der Kolk, 1996), may become something to be feared and avoided, defensively shutting down sensations and closing off the possibility of intimacy and pleasure with another. For young children, for whom touching and being

touched are essential building blocks for a healthy relationship to themselves and others, the recovery of trust in one's body and the body of the caregiver is an essential component of developmental progress.

The intervention must give the message that one can safely touch and be touched, and that the pleasure of safe touching is something to be cherished. This message can be given by encouraging expressions of affection between the parent and the child, by accepting naturally but without excessive enthusiasm the expressions of physical affection of the child to the therapist, and by not recoiling from casual physical contact in the context of play or other activities.

5. *Restoration of reciprocity in intimate relationships.* If the loss of a secure base is the earliest and most damaging consequence of psychological trauma, its reconstruction is essential to recovery. Secure attachments are built on the caregiver's ability to respond contingently to the young child's signals (Ainsworth et al., 1978). Conversely, violence-related traumatization involves the most extreme disruption of mutuality through the creation of helplessness in one partner by the domination of the other (Benjamin, 1988). Battered women are often impaired in their ability to foster an emotionally reciprocal relationship with their children because of emotional numbing and hyperarousal, which may lead them to ignore or overreact to their children's behavior. Children exposed to violence, for their part, may engage in internalizing and externalizing behavioral problems that are likely to exacerbate the mother's maladaptive responses. The intervention must involve a search for solutions to failures of reciprocity that are both developmentally appropriate and within the scope of the psychological resources of the parent and the child.

The child–parent therapist must also attend to failures of reciprocity that flow from the complicated and sometimes very different feelings that the battered mother and her child experience toward the father. Both of them may alternately fear and love him, and, if he is gone, yearn for his return. But they may not experience these feelings at the same time or with the same intensity. Failures of reciprocity can occur when the child is longing for the father's return at a time when the mother is focused on her fear of him and her need to protect herself and her child from him. The intervention must involve the search for resolutions to these lapses of reciprocity, helping the parent and child understand one another's perspectives.

6. *Normalization of the traumatic response.* Traumatized adults often worry that they are "crazy;" children harbor fantasies that they are "bad" and "unlovable" when their behaviors evoke negative responses from others. Both may feel guilty because they could not stop the traumatic event from occurring or because they harbor sometimes very graphic and violent wishes for revenge. For adults as well as for children, treatment focuses on establishing a frame of meaning and validating the legitimacy and universality of the traumatic responses. Revenge fantasies can become manageable when they are reframed as an understandable desire to restore a feeling of fairness by undoing the painful consequences of an aggressive act.

7. *Encouraging a differentiation between reliving and remembering.* Being flooded by intrusive recollections is one of the frequent sequelae of trauma. In children, it is manifested in repeated reenactment of the traumatic scenes either through action or through play. Treatment involves helping the adult or the child realize the connection between what they are doing and feeling in the moment and the traumatic experience, stressing the difference between the past and present circumstances, and increasing the person's awareness of the current, safer surroundings.

8. *Placing the traumatic experience in perspective.* Treatment focuses on helping the adult or the child to gain control over the uncontrolled emotions evoked by the memory of the trauma. Children and adults are encouraged to achieve a balance where the memory of the trauma is not eradicated, but there is a marked decrease in being preoccupied by it. Instead, the person is encouraged to take pleasure in rewarding life events and personal characteristics, and to make space to appreciate the positive and enriching aspects of life.

Intervention Modalities in Child–Parent Psychotherapy

A particular challenge for child–parent psychotherapy is that the intervention goals and mechanisms of change previously described need to be cultivated simultaneously for two partners (parent and child) who are at different developmental stages and who, as a result, process the experience of violence differently. Sometimes paradoxically, child–parent psychotherapy relies on the traumatized (and sometimes abusive) parent to be an active partner in the process of promoting the psychological healing of the child. When both parents as well as siblings are present, the challenge is even greater because the needs of several participants must be taken into account. Nevertheless, the difficulties of this approach are more than compensated by its therapeutic potential because healing the child–parent relationship holds the promise of individual healing both for the parent and for the child (Lieberman & Van Horn, 1998). A growth-promoting child–parent relationship can then support the ongoing healthy development of the child long after the intervention itself has ended.

As described in the previous section, the goals and mechanisms of treatment for trauma are characterized by the belief that the negative effects of trauma in infancy and early childhood can be relieved when the child is able to integrate body-based sensations, feeling, and thinking into a growing under-standing that:

- Stressful bodily experiences can be alleviated through the help of others and through active coping strategies on the child's part;

- Adults can support and protect the child from danger and fear;

- The child is not to blame for the frightening events that occurred;

- Strong negative feelings can be talked about instead of enacted; and

- Life can contain elements of pleasure, mastery, and hope.

Child–parent psychotherapy makes use of six major intervention modalities to accomplish these goals. Within each modality, there is emphasis on legitimizing the affective experience and promoting a sense of competence in both the parent and the child. The six intervention strategies are described here.

Promoting Developmental Progress Through Play, Physical Contact, and Language

Healthy development in the early years is based on the child's ability to engage in trusting relationships, explore and learn, contain overwhelming affect, clarify feeling, and correct misperceptions. Sensitive responsiveness to the child's signals, safe and supportive physical contact, age-appropriate play, and the use of language to explain reality and put feelings into words are basic com-petence-building strategies to promote these capacities. These strategies are even more crucial for infants, toddlers, and preschool children whose behavior is dys-regulated and whose perception of relationships is damaged as the result of exposure to violence. Play and language are used as vehicles to explore themes of danger and safety and to build a vocabulary for feelings that can replace the child's use of destructive action to express anger, fear, and anxiety. The books *Your Child at Play* (Segal, 1998a, 1998b) are a valuable resource for clinicians who want to learn how to encourage age-appropriate play activities geared to children from birth to 5 years of age.

Offering Unstructured Reflective Developmental Guidance

This intervention modality provides the parent with information about age-appropriate children's behavior, needs, and feelings as these emerge spontaneously in the course of the sessions. The therapist links the child's behavior, needs, and feelings to the circumstances of the family's life and how these circumstances, including witnessing domestic violence, may influence the child's experience. The developmental guidance is "unstructured" because it does not follow a prescribed curriculum, and it is "reflective" because it promotes "reflective functioning" (Fonagy, Gergely, Jurist, & Target, 2002) by encouraging the parents to attend to their own internal experiences as well as to how their children are likely to understand and respond to a particular situation.

An unstructured and reflective approach to providing developmental information is individually tailored to the particular impasses, struggles, or conflicts that emerge in the child, the parent, or their relationship in the course of the intervention. It also addresses areas of pleasure, competence, and mastery. Whenever possible, the parent's own life experiences are used to frame the developmental guidance and increase the parent's understanding of what the child might be going through. Information and reflection about developmental processes, reframing, empathy, and appropriate limit-setting are emphasized in this modality.

Providing developmental guidance involves not only giving information but also helping the parent appreciate young children's construction of the world (Fraiberg, 1959; Lieberman, 1993). Twelve common developmental themes are listed here.

1. Crying and proximity seeking are the small child's most basic communication tools, and children develop a healthy sense of compe-

tence and self-esteem when the parent responds by offering comfort.

2. Young children have a strong desire to please their parents, although parents are often unaware of it.

3. Separation anxiety is an expression of love and fear of loss rather than a manipulative ploy.

4. Young children fear losing their parent's love and approval.

5. Young children imitate their parents because they want to be like them.

6. Children blame themselves when their parent is angry or upset or when something goes wrong. This tendency is an emotional byproduct of the cognitive egocentrism of young children, which leads them to overestimate their role in the relation between cause and effect (Piaget, 1959).

7. Young children believe that the parents are always right, know everything, and can do anything they wish. This belief in the parents' omnipotence goes hand in hand, often paradoxically, with children's belief in their own power and their determination to assert it.

8. Children feel loved and protected when parents are confident about their child-rearing practices and enforce their rules about what is safe and what is dangerous, right and wrong, allowed and forbidden.

9. Toddlers and preschoolers use the word "no" as a way of establishing a sense of autonomy, not out of disrespect for the parents.

10. Babies and young children remember. They have well developed memories from an early age, and their capacity to remember precedes their capacity to speak about their memories. Memory is particularly vivid for events that evoke strong emotions, such as joy, anger, or fear. The memories may not be completely accurate because they are influenced by the child's affective state and cognitive level, including their understanding of cause–effect relations. Children are keen observers of what happens around them and may remember it for a long time afterward.

11. Babies, toddlers, and preschool children feel intensely, but don't yet know how to regulate their emotions. Intense crying, tantrums, and aggression are not expressions of the child's intrinsic nature, but manifestations of distress that the child is too immature to express in socially acceptable ways.

12. Conflicts between parents and children are inevitable due to their different goals, personalities, and developmental agendas. Conflicts can serve a valuable developmental function when they are used to highlight the separate but equal legitimacy of the partners' goals and wishes, and to mobilize collaboration for the purpose of resolution.

These common developmental themes come as a surprise to many parents, but most particularly to parents whose upbringing has been characterized by stress, pain, and unpredictability. In learning how their children interpret the world, parents often find new meaning in their childhood memories, and in this process they can acquire a richer and more compassionate understanding of themselves.

Modeling Appropriate Protective Behavior

This modality involves taking action to stop dangerously escalating behavior, such as retrieving a child who is engaged in self-endangering behavior or stopping a child from hurting others. Modeling by the clinician is always followed by an explanation about the reasons for the action and an invitation to the parent (and the child, if it is appropriate) to reflect on what happened and to understand the danger potential and the importance of protective action. Emphasis is placed on how much the parent and the child care for each other, and how important it is to be safe from danger. The clinician also models appropriate protective behavior geared to the parent's safety by outlining sources of concern and suggesting alternatives when the adult engages in risky activities.

Interpreting Feelings and Actions

At its best, interpretation allows the parent and the child to experience an increased sense of inner and interpersonal coherence by giving meaning to disorganized feelings and inexplicable responses and behaviors. In this sense, interpretation involves speaking about the unconscious, unspoken, or symbolic meaning of the parent's or the child's behavior in a way that increases self-understanding in the parent or the child.

A frequent form of interpretation in child–parent psychotherapy is making explicit the links between the parents' perception of their life experiences, their feelings for their children, and their parenting practices. For example, parents who were routinely physically punished, criticized, and neglected may unconsciously repeat these patterns in relation to their children (Fraiberg, 1980;

Lieberman & Pawl, 1993). In cases of domestic violence or maltreatment, the battered parent may see an unsettling resemblance between the child and the abusive partner or an abusive caregiver from the past, or may view the child's motives or behavior through the lens of trauma and anticipate aggression and victimization. In these cases the parent might make negative attributions that are internalized by the child and deeply influence the child's sense of self (Lieberman, 1999; Silverman & Lieberman, 1999).

Using timely interpretations can help parents become aware of the unconscious repetition of their past in the present, correct their distorted perceptions of the child, and free them to learn developmentally appropriate child-rearing practices. Interpretation can also help the child become more aware of maladaptive unconscious beliefs and defense mechanisms.

Interpreting unconscious processes calls for utmost tact and a well-honed sense of timing. This is particularly the case when the therapist feels the need to interpret the parent's behavior in the presence of the child. In the case of preverbal, presymbolic infants and toddlers, interpreting the parent's behavior can usually take place in the child's presence because the child, not having mastered receptive language, is less likely to be burdened by an understanding of the parent's painful experiences. Older toddlers and preschoolers present a challenge to the use of interpretation geared to adults because they claim greater participation in the therapeutic interaction, and because they have greater understanding of what the parent and the clinician are saying (Lieberman, 1991).

Speaking in front of the child about highly emotionally charged topics can compound the child's stress and worry about the parent's and child's safety and well-being. Conversely, many children are routinely exposed to inappropriately difficult topics because adults often carry on conversations as if children were not present or were unable to understand what the adults were saying. For children who are present when their parents or other adults discuss disturbing topics, not addressing those same topics in the therapeutic setting is tantamount to conveying the message that there are subjects that cannot be discussed with the therapist. In such situations, the clinician faces a difficult dilemma. What is more conducive to the child's mental health? To discuss in her presence topics that are not appropriate for her age as a way of presenting a more balanced view of situations the child witnesses in the course of her daily life? Or, alternatively, to model for the parent a protective stance where children are shielded from topics that are stressful to them?

The answer is usually highly specific to individual situations. As a result, the clinician must weigh whether and when it is appropriate to elicit from the parent information about emotionally laden experiences in the presence of the child. If the clinician decides that speaking in front of the child would be threatening or harmful to the child, three different strategies that involve modifying the dyadic format of the sessions may be used.

- The session may be divided into two sections, one that is adult-centered and the other, child-centered. Such an arrangement is often welcomed by parent–child dyads who find themselves at odds with each other because each wants time alone with the clinician.

- Occasional or regular collateral individual meetings with the parent may be used when direct intervention with the parent is important to bring about improvement in the child–parent relationship and the child's development.

- Referrals for concurrent individual or group psychotherapy can also be implemented when the parent is in ongoing need of such services.

The use of interpretation is often associated with bringing awareness about the origins of negative feelings such as anger and sadness. The model of "ghosts in the nursery" (Fraiberg, 1980) has become the classic representation of the intergenerational transmission of trauma from parent to child through abusive and neglecting relationship patterns. In this model, the child is freed from engulfment in the parental conflicts when the parent is able to gain insight into the early origins of his or her feelings of rejection, anger, and alienation toward the child. It is equally important, however, to help parents identify and integrate into their sense of self forgotten or suppressed beneficial influences in their life experience. These "angels in the nursery" (W. Harris, personal communication, April 23, 2003) serve as harbingers of hope by upholding the possibility of goodness within the parent, the child, and the parent–child relationship (Lieberman, Padron, Van Horn, & Harris, 2004).

Providing Emotional Support/Empathic Communication

All effective therapeutic interventions are built on a foundation of trust that develops through the clinician's emotional availability. In child–parent psychotherapy, parental emotional support and empathic communication with the child are facilitated by the presence of these qualities in the clinician's way of relating to the parent and the child. Supportive and empathic interventions take the form of conveying, through words and action, a realistic hope that the treatment goals can be achieved; sharing in the satisfaction of achieving personal goals and developmental milestones; helping to maintain effective coping strategies; pointing out progress; encouraging self-expression; and supporting reality testing (Luborsky, 1984).

Offering Crisis Intervention, Case Management, and Concrete Assistance With Problems of Living

This modality consists of taking appropriate action to prevent or remedy the consequences of a family crisis or stressful circumstances. Although listed last, this strategy is often the first to be used when intervention begins, because victims of domestic battering are often faced with a variety of real-life stresses that require immediate attention. Helping the parent in concrete ways can be the primary building block in forming a solid working relationship because the parent perceives the clinician as actively involved and receptive to her or his plight. This modality of intervention might involve advocacy for the family with the housing authorities to prevent an eviction, consultation with the child-care provider to prevent expulsion of the child for inappropriate behavior, mediation between the mother and Child Protective Services if questions of abuse or neglect arise, or referral to other needed services.

Families in which there is domestic violence often face difficult legal issues. Child custody decisions, filing and enforcement of restraining orders, dealings with attorneys, depositions, court appearances, and other aspects of the legal system are bewildering in their own right and can be even more stressful for battered women who are suffering from the psychological sequelae of the violence and who continue to fear for their own and their children's safety. Clinicians must be reasonably knowledgeable about the relevant laws and regulations in their states, and they need to provide appropriate referrals as well as assist parents in coping with the stresses inherent in their legal difficulties. This may include assuming the role of advocates and intermediaries in dealing with the legal system when this is necessary to protect the parent's or the child's safety. These issues are discussed more fully in Section III of this manual.

Children exposed to violence often enact their emotional difficulties in the child-care environment. Consultation with the child-care provider, "shadowing" of the child, and promoting communication between the parent and the child-care provider around the child's needs are often integral components of child–parent psychotherapy.

What Is Unique About Child–Parent Psychotherapy?

None of the six individual modalities described above is, in itself, unique to child–parent psychotherapy. The uniqueness of child–parent psychotherapy resides in the integrated use of these modalities, which are flexibly deployed according to the family's needs. In this sense, child–parent psychotherapy is truly cross-disciplinary, combining elements of social work, mental health intervention, teaching, and advocacy.

Two features distinguish how the different therapeutic modalities are used in child–parent psychotherapy.

1. The integrated use of all the modalities toward the therapeutic goal of promoting a more secure and growth-promoting relationship between the child and the parent(s).

2. The selection of each modality, as needed, for the specific purpose of changing the mental representations that the child and the parent have of themselves and of each other, and changing the behaviors through which these mental representations are enacted.

These two features and the general trauma treatment goals already described guide the treatment plan and the choice of intervention modalities. A central principle in our model is that neither empathy nor insight are sufficient in themselves to affect therapeutic change. Empathy and insight need to be linked to appropriate behavior in order to help the child and the parent, both individually and in their relationship to each other.

The integration of different modalities that is the hallmark of child–parent psychotherapy conveys a powerful message to the parent and the child about the therapist's commitment to the totality of their experience. This includes not only problems in feeling and thinking (the conventional loci of mental health intervention) but also everyday dilemmas, concrete circumstances, and problems of living. Such an encompassing therapeutic stance maximizes the chances for the "moments of meeting" (i.e., authentic interpersonal connections that reorganize the way patient and therapist know each other) that add "something more" to psychodynamic interpretations and promote therapeutic change (Stern et al., 1998).

Child–parent psychotherapy is unchanging in its goals but versatile in its choice of therapeutic strategies. Depending on the particular needs of the child and the parent, different intervention modalities can be added to those already described. For example, infant massage can be used to help a motorically disorganized infant achieve better state regulation. Breathing techniques can be used to help a mother in a state of acute anxiety to regain her calm. Therapeutic sessions may be videotaped for joint review in the next session. The decision to introduce these and other interventions is guided by clinical need and by the therapist's repertoire of intervention skills.

As the field of mental health intervention in infancy and early childhood accumulates experience with successful forms of intervention, these strategies will be incorporated to the modalities currently used by child–parent psychotherapy. Referrals to alternative forms of intervention, such as individual psychotherapy for the parent or the child, stress- and anger-management groups, trauma groups, a spiritual community, massage, meditation, exercise classes, and other activities are made on the basis of relevance and appropriateness to the needs of the family.

The versatility of child–parent psychotherapy lends it some resemblance to the multisystemic treatment of antisocial behavior in children and adolescents (Henggeler et al., 1998). Influenced by the seminal contributions of Bateson (1972) and Bronfenbrenner (1979) to the understanding of family systems and social ecology, multisystemic treatment emphasizes the multidetermined nature of serious antisocial behavior. Multisystemic treatment involves the flexible deployment of a variety of intervention strategies designed to target the factors that were jointly identified by the therapist and the family as contributing to the problem. Child–parent psychotherapy shares the philosophy that problem behaviors in children are multidetermined and that intervention must be informed by an understanding of how the multiple systems in which the child and the family are embedded influence each other. However, within this broad ecological perspective, child–parent psychotherapy gives particular salience to the nature of the transactions between parent and child, because primary caregiving relationships are seen as a powerful common pathway through which diverse environmental influences affect children in the first 5 years of life.

Ports of Entry for the Intervention: Building From Simplicity

Different opportunities for intervention call for different intervention modalities that need to be deployed according to the most salient need of the situation. Stern (1995) spoke of "ports of entry" as the component of the child–parent system that is the immediate object of clinical attention—the avenue through which the clinician enters into the system to effect change. Once a port of entry emerges, the clinician must choose the specific therapeutic modality through which constructive change is most likely to occur.

Simple interventions are often the best. Many parents lack elementary developmental information. Once they learn it, they are able to implement it without much trouble. Telling a parent that pediatric advice now recommends that babies sleep on their backs rather than on their tummies in order to prevent sudden infant death syndrome (SIDS) is one example. Most parents need to hear this advice only once in order to heed it. Well-timed information, advice, and showing by example, when offered tactfully and placed in the context of the parent's cultural values, are time-honored methods for helping parents learn rapidly and well.

Only when these methods are not effective should the clinician consider forms of intervention geared to the parent's resistance, mistrust, or other psychological obstacles. Child–parent psychotherapy does not rely on a single, conceptually determined port of entry, such as the maternal representation of the child. Rather, there are various possible ports of entry, and the port of entry is chosen on the basis of the presence, appropriateness, and modulation of child and parent affect. The specific port of entry may vary from family to family or, within a family, from session to session or from one time frame to another within a session. This variety of ports of entry adds versatility, flexibility, and emotional richness to the intervention. Commonly used ports of entry are described here.

1. The child's behavior (e.g., a baby's inconsolable crying or a toddler's tantrum);

2. The parent's behavior (e.g., bitter complaint about not sleeping all night because of the baby's crying or about fatigue for having to keep track of a toddler's whereabouts);

3. The parent–child interaction (e.g., parental unresponsiveness to the baby's frantic screaming or the toddler's self-endangerment; the child hitting the parent in anger);

4. The child's representation of the self (e.g., a preschooler saying "I don't like myself");

5. The child's representation of the parent (e.g., a toddler making the mother doll spank the baby doll; a preschooler saying to the parent: "You don't love me");

6. The parent's representation of the self (e.g., a parent saying: "I was never good at anything");

7. The parent's representation of the child (e.g., a parent saying: "He is a bad seed, just like his father");

8. The child–mother–father interaction (e.g., a child saying to the mother: "When my daddy comes over, I'll tell him to kill you");

9. Inter-parental conflicts regarding the child (e.g., the father saying to the mother that she spoils the child, and the mother replying: "Well, you never pay any attention to him, so I have to give him extra love");

10. The parent–therapist relationship (e.g., a parent not showing up for an appointment, a parent responding to the therapist's description of the treatment program by saying: "Programs are problems");

11. The child–therapist relationship (e.g., a preschooler telling the therapist: "Don't smile at me, you are ugly"; a toddler crying and holding on to the therapist at the end of session, screaming: "no bye, no bye!");

12. The parent–child–therapist relationship (e.g., the parent telling the therapist: "My son likes you better than me.").

This list is by no means exhaustive. Relationships affect each other, thus opening up thousands of possibilities for intervention. The clinician needs to use clinical judgement to determine which port of entry is most likely to be conducive to therapeutic change on the basis of timing and receptiveness of the parties involved.

Regardless of the port of entry selected by the clinician, one guiding principle must always be followed. Whenever speaking directly to the parent or directly to the child, the clinician must keep the parent–child relationship in mind. Even experienced clinicians sometimes make the mistake of focusing on one member of the dyad to the exclusion of the other when first learning to use this model. This unilateral focus of attention can go on for several minutes or for entire sessions, with the result that the parent and child are encouraged to form intimate individual relationships with the clinician rather than cultivate and enrich their relationship with one another. Although the clinician's relationship with the parent and the child is an important vehicle for healing, the child–parent psychotherapist seeks primarily to serve and support the relationship between the parent and the child, and makes that relationship the focus of the intervention. When clinicians choose a port of entry that involves speaking directly to the parent or to the child, it is critical that they consider how the other member of the dyad will hear and experience that intervention. Clinicians who hold both members of the dyad in mind create an atmosphere that promotes emotional proximity between the parent and the child because their relationship is assumed to be chiefly responsible for supporting the child's development.

Intervention and the Child's Developmental Stage: Using Play, Action, and Language

Ports of entry and intervention strategies must be geared to the child's developmental stage. In general, the less verbal the child, the more effective it is to intervene using direct action. An inconsolably crying baby needs to be picked up and soothed; a toddler who is running away needs to be retrieved and held back; a young child who is about to do something forbidden needs to be distracted and redirected to a different activity. Taking effective action does not preclude using language as an intervention tool. For preverbal children, children who are delayed in their use of language, or children who are so wrought up that they cannot pay attention to speech, the adult's use of verbalization is a useful adjunct to action because it helps the child to associate behavior with symbolic meaning. However, unambiguous action is the primary vehicle for intervention in these situations. Whenever possible, the clinician will support the parent in taking action. Where safety demands it, however, the clinician may first take action and then discuss that action with the parent and child.

Although action-based interventions are appropriate for the very young child, the same interventions are insufficient or even inappropriate for an older child who is able to use language. A preschooler must learn to restrain aggressive impulses as a first step in acquiring a reliable moral conscience that enables him to understand that it is wrong to hurt others. For example, a scarcely verbal 24-month-old child can be redirected to bite a teething ring rather than another child when the urge to bite takes over. Much more is expected of a preschool child: a verbally fluent 4-year-old, for example, needs to recognize when the anger is about to spill out into biting, and he must learn to leave the situation or to put the anger into words rather than into biting. He must conjure up the realization, before he bites, that biting hurts and that hurting others is wrong. The interventions for such a child must aim at helping him construct a sense of self in relation to others that includes this sense of moral accountability. For older children, the use of language to explain feelings and how the world works becomes an increasingly salient form of intervention.

Action and language are essential tools that the clinician brings to the therapeutic situation, but the child communicates most freely through play. That is the reason for choosing play as the first domain of the intervention in Section II of the manual. Winnicott (1971) pointed out that psychotherapy involves two people "playing together", in other words, sharing a game without rules in which the players create a spontaneous dialogue with no predetermined goal or conclusion.

In child–parent psychotherapy, it is at least three people who play together: the child, the parent, and the therapist. Turn-taking and giving others the space to play become more complex because the parent may want to direct the child's play or take over the play space. The therapist's role is to be a guardian of the child's freedom to play, facilitating the fluidity of the exchanges and moving tactfully to prevent either the parent or the child from monopolizing or becoming coercive in directing the flow of the play. Optimally, the child and the parent build a new freedom to play both individually and together in child–parent psychotherapy. They find ways of balancing out the urge to be the main actor in the play with understanding and respect for the other's urge to do the same. Through playing together and with the therapist, they learn to take turns without feeling obliterated or abandoned.

The clinician's understanding of developmental stages and individual differences in the early years is essential in guiding developmentally appropriate interventions. There are a number of excellent books and papers that describe early childhood development. Clinicians should strive to integrate this conceptual knowledge with their experience-based knowledge of young children and their parents.

Stages of the Intervention

There is no empirical data to determine the optimal length of an intervention. Traditionally, mental health interventions are conducted for as long as clinically indicated. This means that the intervention continues until there is a consensus between therapist and client that the emotional difficulties that prompted the intervention are less intense and pervasive and can be autonomously managed by the client using the coping skills acquired in the course of treatment. This clinical goal is often tempered by economic considerations, which limit the length of treatment in many situations.

This manual is designed for interventions of weekly sessions for a period of 12 months that take place in the home or in an office playroom and last approximately 1 hour. This average duration may be modified to suit individual circumstances. Parent and child are routinely present during the visit, although individual sessions with the parent may be scheduled to discuss issues that are best addressed privately.

Exceptions may occur when the parents are so unable to collaborate in the treatment on behalf of the child that their presence becomes damaging, for example when the parent routinely monopolizes the session in ways that are overstimulating or overwhelming for the child. In these situations, it is often helpful to conduct separate individual sessions with the child and with the parent until the parent's functioning improves to the point of enabling him or her to engage in joint sessions with the child. In general, the intervention comprises the following three major stages.

1. <u>Establishment of a collaborative process and formulation of the intervention</u> (months 1–3). The first 3 months are devoted to developing a collaborative relationship with the family. The initial sessions often involve a

trial-and-error process where the parents want to talk about what is happening in their lives, a desire that is often thwarted by the child's needs as these are expressed in the moment. At the same time, the child often clamors for the clinician's attention and expresses anger and resentment when the adult and clinician talk with each other to the exclusion of the child.

The clinician's role is to divide attention judiciously, with an eye to encouraging joint activities between parent and child whenever appropriate. A format for the session is collaboratively developed during this stage. The most common format is joint interaction among parent, child, and clinician. However, in cases where the individual claims of parent and child on the clinician are urgent and incompatible, a provisional decision may be reached to divide the session in two components, one where the child is the center of the attention and one where the parent may discuss his or her own concerns while the child engages in autonomous pursuits in the proximity of the adults. This format can change as the intervention progresses and parent and child become more reciprocally interactive with each other.

During this initial stage, the clinician pays close attention to the way the child and parent communicate with each other; how they express positive feeling; and how they manage distress, disagreement, and conflict. On the basis of these observations, the clinician formulates the most salient areas of strength and of difficulty (including punitive parenting and affect dysregulation in parent and child), develops with the parent a shared agenda for intervention, and tests specific intervention strategies. Resistance to the intervention is addressed in a collaborative, nonconfrontational and nondefensive manner.

2. Clarification and targeting of the identified problem areas (months 4–8). The second stage builds on the initial formulation and trial intervention strategies. As effective forms of intervention are identified, the clinician begins putting into words the areas of strength, the problems being addressed, and the solutions found. Parent (and child, when age-appropriate) are encouraged to practice satisfying problem-solving and interactional strategies so that these are learned in lasting ways. Resistance to the intervention continues to be addressed through efforts to understand and address the reasons for it.

3. <u>Recapitulation and termination</u> (months 9–12). The third and final stage involves a gradually decreasing focus on areas of difficulty interspersed with increasing focus on the positive changes that were made, reminiscing about specific experiences together, comparing how things were at the beginning of the intervention and how things are now, and acknowledging that the intervention is approaching its end. Feelings associated with loss as the result of termination (anger, sadness, regret over unfinished business, gratefulness for improvements) are addressed and reflected on.

Loss is a critical issue for adults and children who have experienced traumas. Trauma itself can be considered a loss: in the moment of trauma one loses the assumption that the world is a safe place and that one is worthy of protection when threatened. Termination of treatment is, therefore, a critical milestone. It is important to allow both parent and child to express the many complex feelings that may arise, and to manage termination in a careful and planful way.

For dyads that have achieved their treatment goals, termination may feel like a positive accomplishment, and their feelings of sadness at saying good-bye may be mingled with real feelings of pride and eagerness to move forward on their own. For these dyads, the last session may take on an air of celebration, with refreshments and, if appropriate, photographs taken on the spot to mark the occasion as a special event. Other terminations might have a less optimistic feel. The treatment may terminate because, for example, the therapist has reached the end of the training year and must move on or because the agency at which the parent and child are being seen offer time-limited treatment. In these cases, it might be a mistake to force an air of celebration at the end of the treatment. In any case, termination must be managed with utmost care. How the last session will be marked is something to be discussed collaboratively among the clinician, the parent, and the child.

The Intervention Setting: Office Playroom or Home Visiting?

Child–parent psychotherapy can be conducted in a variety of settings. The two most frequent settings are the office playroom and the home, and each of these settings has its advantages and limitations. When the treatment is conducted in an office playroom, the predictability of the setting serves as a safe container in which the parent and child can enact their difficulties and practice more adaptive conflict-resolution strategies without external distractions. At the same time, many of the immediate stresses that impinge on the day-to-day child–parent relationship may remain unnoticed and unaddressed.

Home visiting, however, has a different set of advantages and disadvantages. Home visiting can be a remarkably effective vehicle for intervention for at least three primary reasons. First, it reaches out to parents who lack the internal or external resources to come to the clinician's office. Second, it provides an unparalleled opportunity to understand and appreciate the family's circumstances and the child's environment. Third, it gives the parents the message that the clinician is willing to share in their circumstances, however strained they might be (Fraiberg, 1980). As a result, it is not surprising that there is solid empirical evidence supporting the effectiveness of home visiting as a format for intervention (Olds & Kitzman, 1993).

Although offering unique opportunities, home visiting also presents special challenges. One primary challenge is how to maintain a focus on the clinical goal in the face of often changing external circumstances. In this sense, home visiting calls for remarkable self-discipline on the clinician's part because what happens in the home is completely unpredictable, from the time of the home visitor's arrival to the time of departure. Such unpredictability starts from very concrete questions prior to the beginning of the visit (How will traffic be at that time? Will there be a parking space? Will the family be there, and if not, how long should one wait? How safe is the neighborhood, and what should one say if a neighbor asks about one's identity and reason for being there?), and continues throughout the visit, which might pose such dilemmas as what to do if one is offered food or drink, how to respond to cultural traditions such as the custom of removing one's shoes at the door, or what is the appropriate response if unexpected visitors are present, if the TV is loudly on, or if the parent spends a large portion of the session talking on the phone.

These questions and dilemmas highlight the first task of home visitors: finding a balance between their identity as professionals with a particular set of goals in mind, and their simultaneous role as guests in the parents' home. The inherent tension between these two disparate social roles is at the root of much uncertainty about what constitutes appropriate clinician behavior during a home visit. As professionals, the home visitors need to tactfully take the lead in shaping what is happening during the session. As guests, they need to respect and abide by the parents' sense of what is appropriate or inappropriate in their home.

If the professional identity prevails, the home visitor runs the risk of coming across as authoritarian, unfeeling, and rude, as if saying, in effect: "When I am in your home, this living room becomes my office and I decide what needs to be done" (and, for example, unilaterally turning off the TV). Such an approach takes away from the parents their sense of dignity and psychological authority over their surroundings, and reduces them to the status of children who must be told what to do in their own homes.

If, however, the home visitor overemphasizes the social aspects of the situation, there is a risk of forgetting the reason for the home visit. Coffee drinking or partaking of a snack can then become a social occasion, rather than a social ritual that signals hospitality and cordiality as the byproduct of a professional relationship, rather than as an end in itself. These tensions can be discussed with the parent during the early stages of treatment so that both the intervenor's and the parent's expectations are clarified and conflict can be resolved in a collaborative way.

Each home visitor must find a personal balance between the professional role and the social role, but doing so calls for self-scrutiny and an empathic awareness of the parents' experience in having a visitor in their personal space. Some clinicians have no qualms about helping a parent wash the dishes, sweep up rice spilled from a box, or participating in hanging the laundry while simultaneously pursuing the goals of the intervention. Other home visitors dislike doing these chores in their own homes, let alone in someone else's, and are punctilious about not participating in everyday routines in their clients' homes. Such variability is inevitable, but respect for the parents' authority in their own home is an essential ingredient of effective intervention.

Clinician Safety

Clinician safety is a central question in determining the appropriate location of the intervention. Prior to establishing whether the sessions can take place in the home, it is important to discuss the issue of safety with the parent whenever there is uncertainty about the neighborhood or the home circumstances. Many parents are only too aware of the danger in their surroundings, and are appreciative of the clinician's candor and explicit reliance on the parent's input.

This is particularly crucial when domestic violence is a problem, even if the perpetrator is no longer living in the home but might still have access to it or has stalked the partner or violated restraining orders in the past. In raising the question of safety, the clinician is modeling an initial attitude of protectiveness toward herself, the parent, and the children that will be demonstrated repeatedly in the course of the intervention.

On occasion, a clinician's deep commitment to the family and to the therapeutic process may result in his or her overlooking or minimizing clues to danger in the environment. Other times, the clinician may be keenly aware of the danger but decide to brave it as a form of solidarity with the client. Such situations can be understood as "parallel processes" where the clinician risks self-endangerment through identification with the endangered parent. When this happens, the clinician is missing an opportunity to demonstrate to the client that it is possible to take decisive action to avert violence and protect oneself and one's children.

Programs that address domestic violence must create an atmosphere of trust where clinicians can disclose their fears, anger, and anxiety to each other, and colleagues can feel free to be outspoken when issues of safety are at stake. Reflective supervision, staff meetings, and weekly case reviews need to be used as a forum to bring up clinical difficulties as well as worries about possible danger. Changing the site of the intervention from home visiting to an office-based setting in order to forestall danger can be the clinician's most eloquent expression of commitment to safety as an overriding goal of the treatment.

Alternative Settings

Sessions can be conducted in settings other than the home or the office playroom. Beleaguered and disempowered families often need help with transportation for important appointments or in running errands essential to the household. Assistance with problems of living involves the clinician's willingness to help out in these matters. When this happens, the car, the street, the supermarket, the pediatrician's waiting room, or the housing authority offices may become settings for the intervention.

A therapeutic setting can be defined most succinctly as any place where the parent, the child, and the clinician spend time together and interact with each other because any of these settings can offer the opportunity for transformative action. At the same time, the question of clinical focus should guide the reliance on alternative settings as adjuncts to the intervention. The clinician must be aware of the danger that running errands or helping with concrete problems can easily become ends in themselves, blurring the clinical goal of achieving sustained improvement in the parent–child relationship and the child's emotional functioning.

The Role of Cultural Factors in the Intervention

Intimate relationships are regulated by cultural mores, which dictate if, how, and when feelings can be displayed. This is the case for intimate relationships between adults as well as between adults and children. All intimate relationships exist in a cultural context that influences their expression. All cultures have developed mechanisms to contain and modulate the expression of emotions that, left unchecked, can become destructive to the social fabric.

Anger is such an emotion. Different cultures have different tolerance levels for the expression of anger, the channels used to express it, and the people toward whom it may be expressed. An action that is considered violent in one society may well be seen as a normative expression of displeasure in another. This does not mean that a specific culture can be equated with a specific, monolithic attitude toward the expression of anger or any other emotion. Cultures are nuanced and multifaceted, with a wide range of individual differences within a culture. We would be stereotyping a culture if we made sweeping generalizations that did not allow for intracultural differences, which may be due to a diversity of factors including, among others, ethnicity, socioeconomic status, educational background, acculturation, generational differences, age, temperamental style, and family history.

Clinicians must strive to learn about the cultural traditions of the families they work with, and to understand how specific child-rearing practices give expression to the prevailing values of a cultural group. At the same time, this basic stance might have to be modified under certain conditions. For example, there might be child-rearing practices that are common in a particular cultural context but not legally or morally acceptable in the United States. Such practices need to be addressed in the course of the intervention. The fact that they are culturally normative in a different country does not exempt these practices from thoughtful discussion about their function and their effects on the child as seen from the perspective of prevailing values in the United States.

Cultures and the individuals who represent them evolve over time in response to changing circumstances, and they can become more or less tolerant or intolerant of diversity as the result of historical processes and social and economic change. The changing social status of women, children, and minorities are cases in point. These groups have been historically the targets of violence and abuse, but their position within different cultures has changed, both for better and for worse, as the cultures have changed over time in response to historical, sociological, political, and economic circumstances.

A decrease in aggression from those in power toward the less powerful is a moral and therapeutic goal that transcends narrowly defined cultural considerations. Cultural sensitivity should not become a reason for a cultural relativism that condones the infliction of pain by the strong on the weak. In the United States, there is a social consensus that domestic violence and harsh physical punishment of children are harmful and often against the law. From this perspective, neither practice can be overlooked by the clinician or dismissed as an expression of cultural tradition.

When the clinician believes that a parent's child-rearing practice is harmful, the intervention can be couched in an acknowledgement that different cultures have different child-rearing practices. This can be followed with a conversation where the clinician explains why the practice in question is not acceptable in this country and elicits the parent's viewpoint so that the topic can be thoughtfully considered in all its complexity. In elucidating the cultural roots of a specific child-rearing practice or value, clinicians must remember that there is much intra-cultural variation in child-rearing, not least as the result of socioeconomic factors, and that intra-cultural differences may exceed cross-cultural differences in this area (van IJzendoorn & Kroonenberg, 1988). If necessary, a referral to child protective services should be made to protect the child.

The Importance of Counter-Transference Reactions

Working with people traumatized by violence evokes strong emotional reactions in the treatment provider. This is particularly the case in work with young children, who, whether or not they have experienced traumas, are relatively unmodulated in their expression of affect. In addition, young children are unable to protect themselves and must rely on their parents and other adults to be safe and to thrive. Faced with this combination of circumstances, the clinician is likely to experience a range of intense emotions, including rage at the parent, wishes to adopt the child or other rescue fantasies, emotional numbness, physiological responses, and feelings of incompetence and helplessness. Many of these responses mirror the typical symptoms of posttraumatic stress disorder, and may be considered as a vicarious traumatization of the clinician through exposure to narratives or visual images of the violence. Many clinicians have gone through experiences similar to those they are now treating. Bearing witness to the trauma narratives of young children and their parents and helping to contain children's strong feelings may re-evoke earlier traumatic responses. Clinicians may also become enmeshed in the expectations of victims of traumatic violence by a process of projective identification. It is not unusual for those who have been victimized to see others, including the clinician, as potential sources of danger. Clinicians may find themselves acting out the aggressive motivations that have been projected onto them by setting overly rigid limits in the treatment or by aggressive interpretation or confrontation.

Counter-transference experiences are valuable guides to understanding the clinical process. It is not uncommon for a clinician to actively dislike the parent, the child, or both of them. The clinician may dread the next session, feel relief when the parent cancels or does not show up, and wait impatiently for a session to end. If these clinician responses do not change in the course of treatment, it is safe to conclude that no improvement is taking place in the child and parent functioning. The move from disliking to liking the parent and the child is a valuable indicator of therapeutic change.

The clinician's reactions need to be carefully attended to in order to protect the clinician's personal well-being and professional effectiveness. Reflective supervision, with sufficient time allotted for an examination of the clinician's experience, is an integral component of best practice in providing services to families exposed to violence. This process needs to be safe and confidential to enable the clinician to own up to negative feelings and experiences of incompetence without fear of punitive responses on the part of the administration.

Reflective supervision should not be limited to beginning practitioners; it must be built in as an integral component of the clinician's practice, with peers providing supervision and support for each other and serving as sounding boards in situations of uncertainty and stress. It is important to note that the process of supervision may parallel in many ways the process that is taking place in the intervention. A clinician who feels helpless in the intervention might, for example, evoke feelings of helplessness in the supervisor. Careful attention to the supervisory process can often give accurate clues as to how well the treatment is progressing.

Contra-Indications to Child–Parent Psychotherapy in Violent Situations

This manual is designed for use in situations where a baseline of physical safety for the victim of domestic violence and for the child is already relatively well established, even if sporadic threats remain to the overall stability of the situation. Ensuring physical safety is the single most important step in intervention and its highest priority. This may entail referring the victim of domestic violence (most often the mother) to specialized counseling, shelter, and legal services. Intervention with victims of current domestic violence and intervention with perpetrators are highly specialized endeavors that are outside of the scope of this manual.

As a rule, child–parent psychotherapy is not recommended when there is ongoing domestic violence because conducting child–parent psychotherapy in these circumstances can be seen as condoning or colluding with a dangerous situation. In general, when there are no services in place that are specifically geared to the victimizing and victimized adults, it is recommended that child–parent psychotherapy be reserved for situations where the victim of domestic violence and the child have left the dangerous setting and are in a physically safe environment. Exceptions to this rule call for very careful and ongoing clinical evaluation of the frequency and intensity of the violence, the alternative or additional services that need to be included, the adults' motivation to stop the violence, and the effectiveness of the intervention in bringing about a substantial decline in the level of violence.

SECTION II

UNIQUE AND ESSENTIAL ASPECTS OF CHILD–PARENT PSYCHOTHERAPY

THIS SECTION DESCRIBES INTERVENTIONS that are unique and essential to child–parent psychotherapy geared to child's responses to violence in the first 5 years of life. The behavioral/representational domains of intervention are organized in terms of their developmental salience. Very young infants, who have not yet developed a coherent organization of the attachment system, tend to respond to stressful and traumatizing conditions with sensorimotor disorganization and disruption of biological rhythms. As the child develops and organizes responses to danger in relation to the attachment figure, interactional behaviors involving proximity- and contact-seeking, avoidance, resistance, and aggression become increasingly salient, although sensorimotor disorganization and disruption of biological rhythms may persist. Among older toddlers and preschool children, who are increasingly capable of mental representation, language and symbolic play become vehicles for the expression of affective experience and their construction of reality. The domains described here should be seen as concurrent and overlapping, with some domains prevailing at different times depending on the child's developmental stage, constitutional characteristics, and environmental supports and challenges.

An intervention manual cannot, by its very nature, address the thousands of individual circumstances that emerge in the course of treatment. The selection of domains and specific intervention strategies were guided by the desire to highlight general intervention principles that need to be honed to fit individual circumstances. The intervention strategies are described as "items" to reflect the nomenclature proposed for manualization by Waltz et al. (1993).

Timing of Specific Intervention Items

The timing of specific interventions is guided by two overarching principles.

1. <u>Try the simplest and most direct intervention first.</u> For example, if providing developmental guidance is sufficient to change inappropriate parental behavior, exploring the childhood origins of this behavior is unnecessary and might be intrusive and inappropriate.

2. <u>Encourage the parent to intervene on behalf of the child whenever possible.</u> Take direct action with the child only if this effort fails or if the circumstances demand it. For example, if a child is about to engage in risky behavior, calling the parent's attention to it might be sufficient to mobilize protective action. If the parent does not respond or if the child is in immediate danger, the clinician needs to act quickly and decisively to protect the child. The intervention items specify forms of intervention that are the hallmarks of child–parent psychotherapy.

In applying the items, clinicians must be aware of the context in which the intervention takes place. Timing, although difficult to define, is essential in clinical practice. The same intervention may be successful or it may backfire depending on when and how it is implemented. In deciding on the timing of an intervention, parameters to consider are:

- The culturally determined values and child-rearing mores of the family,

- The quality and sturdiness of the therapeutic alliance,

- The level and style of the parent's and child's psychological functioning, and

- The mood of the moment in the parent and the child.

These factors are described in greater detail throughout the manual.

Domains of Intervention

This section describes 12 clinical domains that are particularly salient as the focus of the intervention. The items constitute a brief abstract statement describing an intervention strategy, and are followed by clinical vignettes from narrative notes from sessions. The vignettes reflect the work of different clinicians with different levels of training and working with a range of families of diverse backgrounds. The purpose of the vignettes is to illustrate ways of being and responding, and do not intend to model specific phrasing.

Domain I: Play

Play serves multiple functions in development. Through play, children experiment with different approaches to their relationship with other people and their mastery of the world. Erik Erikson proposed that play is the childhood version of a life-long human propensity: setting up model situations to experiment with different ways of controlling reality (Erikson, 1964). In this sense, play is a tool for learning to manage anxiety. It gives children a safe space where they can experiment at will, suspending the rules and constraints of physical and social reality. Play allows children to enter into the minds of other people and to give meaning to their own and to the other's actions, plans, and wishes.

The centrality of play in children's lives makes it a natural vehicle for therapeutic intervention. In his book *Playing and Reality*, Winnicott (1971) went so far as to conceive of psychotherapy as a form of play when he wrote: "Psychotherapy has to do with two people playing together. The corollary of this is that where playing is not possible then the work done by the therapist is directed towards bringing the patient from a state of not being able to play into a state of being able to play" (p. 38).

This statement is particularly relevant to the treatment of young children, for whom play is often the preferred mode of emotional expression and social communication. Children use play to repeat an anxiety-provoking situation, to change its outcome, or to avoid it altogether by changing all the parameters of the situation or choosing a different play theme. The long history of the psychodynamic understanding of play hinges on an effort to understand the symbolic meaning of its content and to then give it verbal interpretation. In this approach, the play content is seen as the symbolic expression of unconscious wishes, and the therapist's role is construed as the translator of these hidden wishes into words for the purpose of bringing them to consciousness (Klein, 1932; A. Freud, 1936/1966).

These approaches, which emphasize interpretation of the underlying measures of play, have in recent years been expanded to include an appreciation for the multiple and overlapping functions of play (Slade & Wolf, 1994). The importance of "simply playing," involving a noninterpretive, collaborative enterprise between child and therapist, has been persuasively described as a way of helping children to build psychological structures and to make meaning of their experience (Slade, 1994). "Simply playing" serves simultaneous functions, among them: (a) developing a narrative that brings together fragmented, disorganized, and incomprehensible elements into a more-or-less coherent pattern; (b) integrating affect into the narrative in order to promote modulation and integration of affect; (c) promoting a therapeutic relationship in which the child is able to communicate a range of feelings and experiences to the therapist; and (d) developing self-reflection by stepping outside the play and finding meaning in it as a joint enterprise between child and therapist (Slade, 1994).

Overwhelming anxiety that cannot be contained in the play sequence leads to a disruption of play, and this disruption provides a useful clue to the child's inner experience (Erikson, 1964). When the child is traumatized, the character of play becomes driven, so that the child may repeat again and again the concrete representation of the traumatic scene without gaining relief from an increased mastery of it or from the ability to move from concrete to symbolic levels of representation (Gaensbauer, 1995; Terr, 1991). In these situations, "simply playing" is the first step toward helping the child contain overwhelming affect, tell the story, and convey the unspeakable horror of it to someone who understands and protects.

Child–parent psychotherapy builds on these functions of play by encouraging play between the parent and the child. This is particularly useful in the case of traumatized children. Because young children rely on their parents for safety and protection, it is of the utmost importance that the *parent* (and not just the therapist) understands the meaning and impact of the trauma on the child. For young children, the joint meaning created with the therapist in individual psychotherapy is incomplete because this meaning is not available to the child's most important organizer of psychological experience—the parent.

Play functions differently as a therapeutic modality in child–parent psychotherapy than in individual psychotherapy. Both therapies rely on play to access the child's inner world, but in child–parent psychotherapy the clinician shares his or her knowledge of that world with the parent. This sharing enables the parent, alone or together with the therapist, to join in the child's play and to help the child construct different, more adaptive meanings of people and experiences.

There is no substitute for witnessing the child at play as a means to fully understanding how the child experiences the world and the important people in it. In joint parent–child sessions, the child–parent psychotherapist serves as a mediator between the child's play and the parent's understanding of it. The therapist's role, in this sense, is helping the *parent and the child* create joint meaning by playing together and, when timely, stepping out of the play and reflecting on it. This process involves helping the parent tolerate the painful affects and internal representations that the child conveys through play for the purpose of a more real, less dismissive and idealizing portrayal of the way things are for the child. Interpretation of play content is used when both the parent and the child are able to move from enacting to reflection.

Often the parent is unable to play or to join in the child's play. Other times the child cannot play with the parent but uses the therapist as a partner in play. Some children engage in only solitary play for weeks at a time, rebuffing the parent's or the therapist's efforts to join in. Sometimes the play is chaotic, vague, and disorganized; sometimes it is excessively rigid and constricted, or limited to concrete activities such as cutting and pasting or board games. These variations need to be understood as stages in the development of the child's capacity to play rather than as definitive statements about the capacity of the child and the parent to play together.

When the clinician conveys a conviction that child and parent can find a way of playing together, they most likely will be able to do so. On the way to this goal there may be detours and diversions, which may include periods of individual play between child and therapist, either alone or in the presence of the parent. The underlying intention, however, needs to be the involvement of the parent and child in joint play. A successful treatment outcome is when the child and the parent no longer need the therapist to be with each other in developmentally appropriate and rewarding ways.

Many parents do not know about the importance of play in children's development. They may consider that "just playing" is a waste of time that does not constitute "real therapy." It is advisable to use reflective and unstructured developmental guidance to help the parent understand that play is the vehicle through which children learn, experiment with their realities, and express their feelings.

1. The therapist does not focus exclusively on the meaning of the play for the child, but helps the parent understand how the play explicates the child's experience. When the parent can assume a role in the play or in the narrative it tells, the clinician turns that function over to the parent and assumes a role of facilitating play between the parent and child.

> *Example:* Sandra witnessed her mother being brutally attacked and severely injured when she was 3 years old. At age 4, she is brought to treatment because she is increasingly frightened and withdrawn at school, and is not keeping pace with the classroom activities. Her ability to learn is severely affected, and her speech is much regressed. In joint child–mother sessions, Sandra spends weeks creating again and again an impregnable fortress using the playroom furniture. She hides inside this fortress and does not allow anybody to come inside. The therapist helps the mother understand the protective meaning of the fortress while speaking to Sandra from outside the "walls." As the mother understands, she begins to speak to Sandra about the terrible attack they suffered. With the therapist's encouragement, she also stresses the steps she has taken to make sure she and Sandra are safe. Sandra responds by first opening a crack on the fortress wall, and progressively alternating between coming halfway out of the fortress and inviting the mother in. After several months, she says to her mother: "He came in because I did not close the door on time." The mother understands the daughter's sense of responsibility and self-blame, and says: "You are a little girl. You could not close the door. It is not your fault that I got hurt." After this session, there is a noticeable change in the child's play, and the theme of the fortress is replaced by reciprocal play centered on the doll house, with the child telling the mother how to rearrange the furniture.

2. When the parent resists or cannot tolerate the meaning of the child's play, the therapist creates a space in which the child can tell the story while supporting the parent in observing and participating in the play

in as full a manner as is possible, given the parent's own emotional demands.

Example: Angelo, age 2, is watching silently as his father speaks heatedly about his wife's betrayal, which led to a bitter divorce after a violent physical fight that Angelo witnessed. As the father speaks, Angelo approaches the doll house and begins putting every piece of furniture upside down. He throws the dolls out of the house. The therapist says to the father: "I know you are very angry right now, but I have to ask you to stop and watch what Angelo is doing. He is trying to tell you something." As the father watches, the therapist says: "Angelo, everything is upside down. The mommy and the daddy and the baby fell out of the house." Angelo says: "Baby hurt." The therapist repeats: "Baby hurt?" Angelo hurls the baby across the room. The father says: "Don't hurt the baby." Angelo responds by hurling the father figure across the room. The father says: "Don't do that." The therapist says: "Angelo is telling us how he feels. His whole world fell apart. You are angry, and he is angry and scared." The father says: "He's too little to understand what is happening." The therapist answers: "Too little? He seems pretty eloquent to me. How much more clearly can he show you what is happening?" The father is quiet for a long moment, looking at his son, who is looking at him. Then the father says: "Come here, Angelo." As the child approaches him, the father holds him on his lap and says: "I love you, baby."

Example: Jamala, age 3, ties the therapist's wrists with rope and says: "You are going to jail! You are bad!" In session after session, this game is repeated with minor variations, and always includes insults and curses. The therapist responds by saying that she is scared, that she is not so bad, asking for forgiveness, and in other ways expressing fear, sorrow, and remorse. Jamala is unmoved and continues and escalates the punishment, yet never doing anything that can actually hurt the participants in the play. The mother watches uncomfortably at first but becomes increasingly fascinated by her young child's accurate portrayal of the scenes she saw between herself and her husband. Her efforts to participate are answered by the child's refusal to let her play: "You stay out, Mommy. You are ugly." The therapist speaks to Jamala's anger at her mother because her father went away. Jamala asks the therapist to tie her wrists and to send her to jail. The therapist says: "I will be too sad if you go away. I don't want to do that." Jamala screams: "Do it!" The therapist tentatively does it, checking with Jamala in a stage whisper to see if she still wants this to happen at each step of the play. When Jamala "goes to jail," the therapist and the mother loudly call for her, telling each other how much they miss her. Jamala reenters, smiling, and is greeted with great joy. In one of the sessions, months later, Jamala says to the therapist: "Even when I am angry with you, I love you," and sighs as if realizing something very important.

3. **In child–parent psychotherapy, it is critical that the parent understand and be involved in the narrative that the child is telling through play. The therapist helps the child share this narrative with the parent, so that the parent can assume a rightful role as the child's guide and protector, even if the narrative emerges in sessions that the parent did not attend.**

> *Example:* Lydia, age 4, came for child–parent psychotherapy with her aunt. She had suffered many losses in her short life. Her mother abandoned her to the care of her grandmother when Lydia was 2 years old. One month before Lydia turned 4, her grandmother died after a long illness. Lydia's aunt was herself in poor health, and she sometimes missed sessions. The family valued the therapy, however, and when Lydia's aunt was too ill to come to a session, she would assure that a relative brought Lydia to see the therapist. Lydia's play, in sessions with her aunt as well as in sessions when she was alone with the therapist, was filled with themes of being overly busy, overly burdened, and needing to care for many children. In these play sessions, Lydia was always the caretaker, providing for her aunt, the therapist, and the many baby dolls in the playroom. Both the therapist and Lydia's aunt spoke to how hard Lydia was working, how busy she was, and how much responsibility she had. Lydia spoke of her wish to be "grown so I can buy the food and pay the bills."

In one session, when Lydia's aunt did not come and Lydia was alone with the therapist, Lydia began her play, as usual, busily taking care of the therapist and the baby dolls. As she played, she began to talk about getting ready to go to a party with her boyfriend. She told the therapist, "You will have to stay home with the babies while I'm gone." Then Lydia said, "My boyfriend is here, and we're fighting because he's late. He's mad and I'm mad. He's banging my head on the wall, and I'm crying." Then Lydia turned to the therapist and said, "That's what happened to my mommy when we lived in the big house. I was just a baby and I was scared." The therapist asked Lydia if she told anyone. Lydia said, "They don't know. I can't tell them."

Lydia's aunt came to the next session. The therapist tried several times to introduce the story, but each time, Lydia shot her a threatening glance and said, "Don't talk." In supervision, the therapist talked about how burdened she felt by having a secret that Lydia's aunt did not know. With her supervisor, the therapist reflected on the fact that she was burdened by the secret just as Lydia had been. The supervisor noted that the difference was that the therapist was "grown" and that Lydia was just a little girl, too young to have the responsibility of deciding what to do with such an important secret. The supervisor encouraged the therapist to help Lydia share her secret with her aunt so that her aunt could be aware of the burden that Lydia carried and could help her with it.

In the next session, the therapist watched and listened as Lydia again played that she was caring for her aunt, the therapist, and the babies. The therapist, joined by the aunt, began to question Lydia's assumption of so much responsibility. They noted that she was only 4 years old, too little to have such big jobs. The therapist said that Lydia had some grown up secrets that she had been keeping, too. Lydia looked at the therapist angrily and said, "Don't talk." The therapist acknowledged that Lydia didn't want her to tell the story of what happened with her mom, but said that it was too big and too scary a secret for a little girl to keep to herself. She said, "Your auntie needs to know so she can help you and take care of you." Lydia turned her back on the therapist and her aunt and listened tearfully as the therapist told the aunt what had happened to Lydia's mother, and about Lydia's reluctance to tell anyone. Lydia's aunt listened and then turned to Lydia and said, "Did you think I wouldn't believe you?" Lydia nodded silently. Her aunt said, "Did you think you would be in trouble?" Again, Lydia nodded. Her aunt said, "You aren't in trouble, baby. I believe you. I think it happened just the way you said. Of course you were scared." Lydia sat crying softly for a minute, and then said that she wanted to play. She walked to a bin of toy food and picked up a plastic ice cream cone. She pretended to lick it, bringing it closer and closer to her mouth while she watched her aunt closely. Just before Lydia put the ice cream cone in her mouth, her aunt said, "Don't lick that, baby. It's dirty." Lydia put the cone down, smiling with relief at having been cared for, and then crawled into her aunt's lap.

Domain II: Child Sensorimotor Disorganization and Disruption of Biological Rhythms

This section focuses on sensorimotor disorganization as manifested in frequent, intense and prolonged crying; inability to be soothed; motor rigidity, agitation, or restlessness; head banging; temper tantrums; and other behaviors that denote lack of bodily control. Disruption of biological rhythms are discussed in terms of problems with eating, sleeping, and elimination.

All of these behaviors are common in normally developing children, and are not necessarily associated with traumatic experiences or with parental maltreatment. They are often outgrown as the result of neurophysiological maturation and the acquisition of increasingly effective coping skills. However, while they last, these behaviors can be very distressing to the parents and child-care providers, and they can set the stage for adult misperceptions of the child as willfully annoying or noncompliant. As a result, these behaviors can trigger anger and withdrawal in the caregiver, generating a self-reinforcing aversive cycle of interaction between parent and child. When the behaviors are a direct response to trauma, they tend to last longer, are more difficult to alleviate, and tend to return after abating when stressful conditions reappear.

Regardless of the reasons for the child's behavior, it is helpful to use developmental guidance to explain the possible meanings of the behavior to the parent and to search together for ways of responding that are empathically responsive to the child, support development, and alleviate the problem behavior. If, in this process, it becomes apparent that the parent cannot collaborate in the search for a solution, then the clinician might need to explore the parental negative perceptions of the child and their possible links with the parent's individual experience before a developmentally appropriate intervention can become effective.

ITEMS AND CLINICAL EXAMPLES

1. **When the child's behavior does not respond to the parent's efforts to stop it, the clinician elicits the parent's view of the situation, and engages the parent in searching for an effective strategy for calming the child.**

   Example: Carmen, 5 months old, cries frantically when she wakes up, when her diapers are changed, when she is given a bath, and when she sees unfamiliar people. Her mother feels unable to console her. She has begun to change diapers less often, to give sponge baths, and to avoid going out to minimize situations that might trigger Carmen's crying. When the clinician arrives for this particular session, Carmen has been crying non-stop for about 15 minutes by mother's report. Her face is red and she is sweaty. The mother is holding the child over her shoulder, bouncing her rhythmically, because she read that this is optimal for crying babies. The clinician speaks sympathetically to the mother, telling her that this is a very difficult situation, and offers to hold the child if she needs a break. The mother accepts the offer. Carmen's crying intensifies when her mother transfers her to the clinician's arms. The clinician comments: "You want to be with your mommy, don't you? You like your mom best of all even when you are crying." The mother says, ruefully: "Much good it does me. I can't do anything right for her." The clinician says: "I wouldn't blame myself if I were you. Some babies don't do what one expects of them, and Carmen and you have gone through a

lot when her father used to get violent with you in front of her."
The mother's eyes fill with tears. Carmen continues crying. The
clinician says: "What do you say if we try something different?
Maybe Carmen gets too stimulated if we hold her up and bounce
her. Maybe she needs a lot of quiet. What if we dim the lights and
put her on her tummy and sing to her softly while we pat her
back?" The mother answers: "Nothing to lose." The clinician
asks: "Do you want to do it yourself, or do you want me to do it?"
The mother says: "You do it. I'm too frazzled." The clinician says
lightly that the mother will have to bear with her because she
sings out of tune, and the mother gives a little smile while dim-
ming the lights. The clinician starts humming a lullaby while patting Carmen rhythmically on the back as the child lies on her
tummy on the couch. When the baby's crying begins to subside,
the clinician motions to the mother to take over. The mother does
so, singing with a trembling voice at first, then with more self-
assurance. The clinician joins her softly. After a while, Carmen
falls asleep. The mother says: "What a relief." The clinician says:
"We learned something about Carmen. When she cries, one
thing to try is cutting down on the light and on moving her. She
is soothed by patting but not by bouncing, it seems." Mother listens attentively.

The clinician then asks the mother how she is doing, and mother
speaks about her grief in losing her relationship with Carmen's
father, and her simultaneous fear that he'll resume his violence if
they get back together. The clinician uses this sequence to note to
herself that this mother's ability to soothe her baby breaks down
when she is overcome by her concerns about her personal situation. She does not verbalize this realization because her relationship with the mother is not yet well enough established to make
an interpretation of this type, but she tells herself that she needs
to remember to inquire about the mother's personal experience
on a regular basis as part of the intervention. Before leaving, the
clinician makes use of the mother's improved emotional state to
tell her about the new pediatric knowledge regarding the importance of having babies sleep on their backs to decrease the danger
of SIDS, and encourages the mother to turn the baby over for the
night.

If this incident occurred later in the treatment, when the clinician's relationship with Carmen's mother was better established, the clinician might have gone further after helping to calm Carmen. She might have noted that Carmen, like all babies, is sensitive to the states of mind of her mother. The clinician could then help the mother reflect on whether she is less effective in calming Carmen when she is herself upset. Together, the clinician and the mother could work to help the mother be more observant of her own internal states, and to find ways to calm herself so that she can better help Carmen relax.

2. **When the parent seems at a loss to implement a routine, the clinician provides reflective developmental guidance while expressing support for the parent's concerns.**

Example: The mother of Camila, 8 months old, explains that she needs to go back to work after her pregnancy leave but is worried that Camila will "starve to death" because she does not accept a bottle and insists on breast-feeding only. When the clinician asks about the course of breast-feeding, the mother explains that she has always fed on demand because she believes that breast-feeding is important for bonding, but now this is presenting a problem because of Camila's refusal to be fed by anybody other than her mother. On further enquiry, it emerges that the mother feeds Camila 4 or 5 times per hour, and that they have never been apart. Camila also wakes up several times each night to breast-feed. Lately, the mother tried a couple of times to withhold breast-feeding during the night, and each time Camila "knocked herself out" crying until she fell asleep. The mother felt as if she was "torturing" Camila. The clinician sympathizes with the mother's struggle and suggests that it might be less stressful to introduce Camila to a bottle during the day, when both are more rested. She explains that the mother's milk will have more time to be replenished if there is a longer period of time between feedings, and suggests stretching the length of time between feedings so that Camila gets fuller at each feeding. Mother and clinician speak in detail about the mother's fears that this will displease Camila, and the clinician suggests ways of distracting Camila by introducing activities the child enjoys. She reassures the mother that even if Camila is displeased in the moment, she will learn that she can tolerate the change with her mother's support.

3. **When the parent seems unable to follow a routine to help the child acquire better biological regulation, the clinician asks the parent about the obstacles that stand in his or her way and offers alternatives based on the parent's concerns.**

Example: Bobby, 18 months, screams when he is put to bed. His mother deals with this situation by lying next to him until he falls asleep. This can take between 1 and 2 hours each night because Bobby wakes up whenever the mother tries to get up unless he is in a very deep sleep. The clinician has suggested a night-time ritual of telling Bobby that it is time to go to bed, dressing him in his pajamas, brushing his teeth, reading him a book, turning off the lights, and turning on a musical mobile above his bed while saying "I'll see you in the morning." The mother has been unable to implement any of the components of this ritual. She sounds evasive and out of sorts when the clinician asks how the night-time preparations are working, but she continues to complain about Bobby's crying. The clinician says: "I have the feeling that the suggestions I made are not being helpful. Can we review them to see what is not working?" The mother says: "It's too much trouble to go through all those steps." The clinician says she agrees with the mother that there are a lot of steps, and asks which ones are the most trouble. The mother says: "Just the whole bunch. It feels so artificial." Again, the clinician agrees that it doesn't seem to come naturally to have a nighttime ritual. She asks how the mother used to fall asleep when she was little. The mother says: "I used to stay awake for a long time because I was scared of ghosts. I kept being afraid I would see one, but I couldn't tell my mom because she would whoop me if I made noise." The clinician says that many children and even grown-ups are scared of ghosts, and she asks if the mother is still scared of them. The mother says that she is. The clinician says: "Does staying with Bobby makes you feel safer, instead of being all alone in the house with him asleep?" The mother mumbles "yes" in an embarrassed way. The clinician says: "That's nothing to be embarrassed about. A lot of people have those fears. Would listening to music help you?" The mother says she doesn't know, but agrees it is worth a try.

3. **When the child's behavior becomes unmodulated and out of control, the clinician uses a combination of words and actions to help the child de-escalate to a more modulated state.**

   Example: Robbie, 2 years old, screams when his mother takes his baby brother's milk bottle away from Robbie. His mother says dismissively: "He needs to learn not to take his brother's bottle. He's not a baby anymore." The clinician answers: "He doesn't know that. He would like to be a baby and be on your lap, like his little brother is." Robbie continues screaming. The clinician says to the mother: "Do you mind if I try something?" The mother agrees. The clinician kneels down very close to Robbie and says: "You really want that bottle. Let's look for something else you can have." Robbie looks at her for a moment as he stops crying, then resumes his screaming. The clinician says: "Give me your hand and we will find something else that you want." She takes Robbie's hand and purposely takes him around the room, pointing at different things and naming them in a questioning tone, as if asking whether Robbie wants them. Robbie's crying diminishes. The clinician takes a stuffed animal and cradles it in her arms, saying "Don't cry, baby. Don't cry." Robbie watches her with a sober expression. The clinician helps Robbie cradle the stuffed animal, singing softly. Robbie sits on the floor and starts exploring the animal. The clinician turns to the mother and says: "It is hard for him to share you with his brother. He is not a baby, but he is still little. And I know it's hard for you to take care of two little ones." The mother nods quietly.

Domain III: Child Fearful Behavior

Infants, toddlers, and preschool children routinely experience a bewildering variety of fears. Infants may react with excessive distress to unfamiliar sights or noises, to transitions in routines, and to regular caregiving activities such as bathing or changing diapers. For toddlers and preschoolers, seemingly irrational fears such as fear of the flushing toilet, of the moon falling down, of puppets and masks, and of a monster under the bed intermingle with fears that from an adult point of view appear more readily based in reality, such as fear of being alone, fear of the dark, and fear of loud noises. Much has been written about the relationship of these fears to the young child's rudimentary construction of the world and of his or her place in it, which led Selma Fraiberg (1959) to call this period "the magic years." These developmentally appropriate fears are connected with toddlers' and preschoolers' animistic conception of the world and with the child's struggles against forbidden impulses, "bad wishes," and the ever-present possibility of losing control either of bodily functions or of recently achieved coping skills.

For children whose parents are reliably protective, these normative fears are an essential rite of passage that enables them to test out their beliefs and to do battle with their most forbidden wishes and powerful impulses. Eventually they will establish some kind of truce with them, using the safe and benevolent powers of their parents as allies in the process of learning about the world and about themselves. In contrast, children growing up in violent households cannot rely on their parents for reassurance. They do not know when the parent will protect them and when he or she will become dangerously similar to the monsters they fear. Their construction of reality, to be accurate, needs to incorporate fear of the parents as an essential component of self-protection. Unconditional trust in the parents is foolhardy for children who have seen their parents hurt each other or who have been hurt by them. Vigilance and suspicion are more adaptive in the conditions they live in.

In the treatment of children exposed to violence, the clinician needs to establish a delicate balance between two important objectives: recognizing the legitimacy of the child's fear of the parent, and upholding the legitimacy of the parent's love and wish to protect the child. In child–parent psychotherapy, the parent's presence during the session can bring awkwardness to the process of exploring the child's fear of the parent, because parents may feel hurt, defensive, and offended by the realization that their child is afraid of them. Sometimes the parents, themselves traumatized by violence, are too emotionally numb to actually feel love or an active wish to protect their children. Parents might also feel that they do not have the resources to protect even if they want to do so. In these cases, the therapeutic process must build the parents' confidence in their capacity to love and protect, realistically acknowledging at the same time that their children may wish for more love and protection than the parents are able to offer at the moment. It is of the utmost importance not to provide facile reassurance and not to minimize the child's fear. To protect and enhance the child's mental health, the clinician must support the child's right to feel, even if the feeling involved is pain, and even if the feeling produces pain in the parent.

Fear of the parent is superimposed on the two major developmentally expectable anxieties of the toddler and preschool child: fear of separation and fear of losing the parent's love. For children growing up in nonviolent, stable households, reassurance that the parent will return after a separation and that the parent continues to love the child even when angry are routine events that gradually build in the child an inner conviction that anger and love can (and do) coexist. In violent households, in contrast, the intensity of hatred too often obscures the reality of love. Watching one parent hurt the other, observing uncontrolled expressions of anger, and being physically and emotionally hurt cast doubt in the child's mind on the veracity of the parent's love and reliable presence, and exacerbate fears of being left and being unloved.

Many parents are unaware of that. Fears of separation and of losing the parent's love are developmentally appropriate in young children. Educating them about the emotional meaning of these fears, and their relevance to how their child feels about them, is very helpful in generating parental empathy and support for their children because parents have a greater feeling of self-worth when they realize how important they are to their children.

Sometimes it is not realistic to assuage the child's fears. For children living in perpetually dangerous situations, it is untruthful to assure them that the adults will protect them. Empty promises, particularly from a trusted adult, are damaging to children because they fail to address legitimate emotional responses and teach the child that adults are deceptive. In these situations, the only honest intervention is to tell the child that it is right and proper to be afraid, that the adult is very sad about the frightening state of affairs, and that the adult will try very hard to change things for the better and to get help from others to make the situation as safe as it can be.

ITEMS AND CLINICAL EXAMPLES

1. **When the parent is appropriately responsive to the child's fear, the clinician explicitly supports the parent's behavior.**

Example: Antonio, 20 months, screams when he sees his older brother, age 8, wearing a devil mask and gesticulating wildly in his direction. The mother picks him up and says to the brother: "Take off your mask so he can see that it is you." The brother does not obey and continues making loud noises and frightening gestures. The mother says to Antonio: "That is your brother, you are OK," and then, turning to the brother, says sharply: "Take off your mask right now." The child obeys. The mother says to Antonio: "See? It's your brother. He's just playing." Antonio calms down and stares at his brother with wild eyes. The clinician says quietly to the mother: "You sure know how to help him." The mother looks pleased.

2. **When the parent dismisses the child's fear, the clinician describes the reasons for the child's experience and tries to enlist a more supportive parental response.**

Example: Mabel, age 12 months, has been waking up at night screaming loudly for the past 2 months. The mother is exasperated and says that she lets Mabel cry herself to sleep. The clinician listens to the mother's description and then says: "I can understand how tired you are after working all day, but I think Mabel is worried that you won't be there when she wakes up. After all, her daddy left suddenly. Maybe she is worried that you will leave too." The mother says, defensively: "Maybe she is, but what can I do? If I get up and take care of her, I'll just spoil her. Then she'll never go back to sleep." The clinician asks: "Is there anything in between, so she doesn't get spoiled but knows you are there?" The mother says: "I can talk to her from my bed." The clinician responds: "That sounds like a good idea to me." The mother says humorously: "I am already awake anyway, I might as well try something." Mother and clinician laugh; the clinician adds: "Well, if it works, you'll be able to go back to sleep faster than if she continued to cry."

3. **When the parent cannot come up with ideas to alleviate the child's fear, the clinician offers suggestions that are framed in the developmental meaning of the child's behavior.**

Example: Khalil, age 3, has become scared of monsters. He says: "The tiger and the monster will come and eat me." His mother says: "I keep telling him that monsters don't exist, but he is still scared of them. He doesn't believe me." The clinician says: "I think he wants to believe you, but his fear is so strong that he can't. Most children at this age believe in monsters. He wants you to believe that his monsters are real." The mother says: "But they are not real." The clinician says: "You know how some things can be real for us but not for others? That is how it is with children. They really believe in monsters and see them in their imagination. How about if you tell him that you will make sure the monsters don't ever come close to him because you will scare them away?" Amused, the mother says: "I can do that." The clinician encourages the mother to tell this to Khalil. The mother says to Khalil: "I will kick the tiger and the monster out so they can't eat you." Khalil asks: "How?" Hesitating, the mother says: "I will lock the door." Khalil asks again: "And what else?" The mother answers: "I will lock the windows." Khalil asks: "Will you say: Go away, bad monster, don't bother my little boy?" The mother promises she will say that. Increasingly enjoying the exchange, Khalil and his mother continue in this way for a while before Khalil changes the topic, clearly satisfied that his mother will take effective action to protect him.

4. **When the parent does not notice the child's anxious or fearful behavior, the clinician brings it to the parent's attention and encourages the parent to reassure the child about the parent's willingness and ability to protect.**

Example: Angela, age 7 months, starts screaming when she sees a man wearing dark sunglasses and a hat in the hallway of their apartment building. Her mother pays no attention. The clinician asks: "What do you think is making her cry like that?" The mother shrugs and says: "I have no idea." Puzzled by the child's persistent crying, the clinician insists: "Does she know that man? She started crying when she saw him." The mother says: "Yeah, he's a neighbor, but he never dresses like that." The clinician says: "Maybe she doesn't recognize him." The mother replies: "Her daddy sometimes wears a hat and glasses like that, to look cool." After a silence, she says: "Matter of fact, he was looking like that when I threw him out." The clinician asks: "Do you think Angela is remembering the fight and that is why she is crying?" Surprised, the mother says: "Can they remember at this age?" The clinician says: "They sure can." The mother looks thoughtful. She then hugs Angela tightly and says: "It'll be OK, baby, shhh, shhh," as she rocks her.

5. **When the child expresses fear of the parent in a disguised form, the clinician clarifies for the parent the meaning of the child's behavior, and supports the parent in relieving the child's fear.**

> *Example:* Mario, age 4, is playing with the kitchen set and says to his mother: "Look, Mommy, here is the knife of my dream." He then tells the clinician that he had had a "very, very bad dream." She asks him what the dream was about, and he says that the knife was in the dream. He adds: "There was this mommy, no, this monster, and he had this gray knife, just like this one, and it cut me right here, it cut out my heart." He dramatically enacts how the monster cut out his heart with a knife. The mother asks if she was in the dream, and Mario replies that she wasn't, that he wanted her to be there to help him, but she wasn't. The therapist says that it sounded like it was a very scary dream, and Mario agrees that it was. The mother explains that during the dream, he was screaming in his sleep, that she could not wake him up from it, that she had never seen him so upset, and that he slept in her bed for the rest of the night.

> This episode needs to be put in context. Mario's mother was one of the women who, during the initial assessment, reported using physical aggression against her husband, and on one occasion she actually threatened him with a knife in front of Mario. Mother and child had never talked about this before. Now the therapist asks the mother: "Are you a little mad at me that there is a knife among the toys here?" The mother replies, "At first I was mad, but then I thought that this is why we are in therapy, because he needs to talk about things, but it makes me feel guilty that I fright-

ened him so much." The therapist says she understands the mother's mixed feelings, and comments that all parents wish they could turn the clock back and do things differently at times. She adds: "Unfortunately one can't turn the clock back, but one can do what you are doing now, which is to try to help Mario make sense of what happened so that he is not so scared by it." The mother turns to Mario and says: "Mario, I think you are thinking of the time that I pulled the knife out at your daddy." Mario looks at her. She adds: "You are too little to understand this, and I will tell you again when you are older, but I was very mad at your daddy and I am very sorry I scared you so much." Mario moves closer to her and says: "Sometimes you get really angry at me, mommy." The mother is taken aback and looks helplessly at the therapist, who says: "I know that when your mommy gets very angry it can be very scary. But your mommy loves you very much, and she will never take out a knife on you, no matter how angry she gets."

The mother has tears in her eyes. She says, "Mario, I love you so much that I am very sorry you saw me do that, and I promise I will never, ever do something like that to you." Mario smiles, turns to the new doctor's kit, and tries all the medical instruments on his mother, his baby brother, and the therapist. When the mother tries to continue talking about the knife episode, he says: "I'm finished with the knife right now, Mommy. You can put it away."

This sequence demonstrates the importance of viewing clinical material through two lenses: the lens of trauma and the lens of attachment and normative development. Mario and his mother, with the therapist's support, had processed Mario's memories about the incident with the knife as fully as he could tolerate at this time. Mario heard and accepted his mother's reassurance that she would never frighten him again in that way, or hurt him with a knife. Mario's play shows that he feels close to his mother and that he is now ready to move on and to play in a way that allows feelings of competence and helpfulness to coexist with feelings of fear. If Mario's mother and the therapist had insisted on staying with the trauma themes, they would have run the risk of overwhelming him.

5. **When the child expresses fear of a situation that is objectively frightening, the clinician encourages the parent to tell the child that those feelings are legitimate and that the parent and the clinician are trying hard to make things safer for the family.**

> *Example*: Khalil, age 3, has supervised visits with his father, but he is scared to go. During one session, he says: "My daddy yells." The clinician repeats, "Your daddy yells?," turning questioningly toward the mother. The mother tells that a few days earlier Khalil's father came by the house in a drunken state and yelled obscenities and threats at her. She called the police, but he was gone by the time they arrived. The mother's attorney has recommended that she ask for a review of the court order for visitation so that it includes mandated participation in an alcohol abuse treatment program, but she urged her to continue taking Khalil to the supervised visits in order to show good faith. The clinician asks: "What can we do to help Khalil feel safer? Did you talk to him about what happened?" The mother says: "No, I thought he was asleep." The clinician says: "It seems like he heard what happened. Maybe his dad's yelling woke him up. I think it will help him if you talk to him." The mother says to Khalil: "Your daddy yells when he drinks too much. He was drinking when he came and yelled outside the window." The clinician adds: "It is very frightening, Khalil, when your daddy yells. It is not right that he scares you like that. Your mommy is trying very hard to make sure that he stops drinking. That is why there is always somebody who makes sure he is not drinking when you go to see him."

Domain IV: Child Reckless, Self-Endangering, and Accident-Prone Behavior

Infants, toddlers, and preschool children who witnessed domestic violence or were themselves the victims of violence often engage in behavior that endangers their safety. Some children seem to lack age-appropriate skills for monitoring the environment for cues to danger, in spite of being at age level in other cognitive skills. Other children seem unable to control overwhelming impulses that lead them to hurt themselves or to put themselves in situations where they can easily get hurt. There is evidence that temperamental proclivities, such as emotional intensity and high activity level, may serve as a backdrop for the development of aggressive responses in response to stressful environmental conditions, although the research has focused on other-directed rather than self-directed aggression in young children.

In young children who have witnessed or experienced violence, self-endangering behaviors are best understood as the result of deprivation from protective caregiving and of premature exposure to danger and violence at an age when the fundamental building blocks of self-protection are established through relationships with caring adults. In this sense, excessive recklessness and self-endangering in the presence of the mother or other reliable caregiver constitute an attachment disorder. The primary function of the attachment system is to promote proximity and contact with the preferred caregiver in situations of uncertainty or danger in order to maximize survival (Bowlby, 1969/1982). Children who are developing normally use the mother figure as a secure base that helps them establish a balance between exploratory and attachment behaviors by serving as a haven to which they return when frightened or in need (Ainsworth et al., 1978). In contrast, self-endangering young children show a distortion of this secure base pattern because they fail to make age-appropriate use of the mother figure as a secure base for protection or as a resource for monitoring environmental cues about danger. Common manifestations involve darting away from the mother in unfamiliar settings, getting lost, and failing to heed the mother's calls by stopping or returning to her side. When hurt or needy, the children tend to ignore or rebuff the mother or strike out against her aggressively rather than to seek comfort from her. In more severe cases, the child may engage in self-biting, self-scratching, and self-hitting. Even very young children sometimes express a wish to not be alive or wanting to die (Lieberman & Zeanah, 1995).

Self-endangering behaviors often co-occur with aggression toward others, presenting the most graphic manifestation of the frequently reported high correlations between internalizing and externalizing problems in young children. Less understood is the fact that self-endangering toddlers and preschool children invariably show concurrent manifestations of anxiety, which can manifest itself in fear of separation, clinging, hypervigilance about the parent's whereabouts (which contrasts with the episodes of sudden bolting away), sleeping problems, intense and prolonged temper tantrums, low threshold for frustration, unpredictable crying, and multiple fears. These anxiety reactions are often overlooked because the accident-prone behaviors and aggression are so compelling that they galvanize the adults' perception of the child.

The seemingly paradoxical coexistence of anxious (fearful) and reckless (danger-encountering) behaviors suggest that self-endangering actions may be a counterphobic defense against danger in children who do not show indications of biologically based conditions, such as hyperactivity, attention deficit disorder, or mental retardation. In children traumatized by violence, the parental failure to anticipate danger and to provide protection, as well as the parental infliction of pain through punitiveness and abuse, create an ongoing insecurity about when danger will befall them. When the parent ignores dangerous situations, minimizes or ridicules the child's fears, entices the child to take risks, inflicts pain, and discounts the experience of pain when the child is hurt, the child's fear and attachment behaviors may be strongly aroused but are not responded to and terminated, thus causing severe distress.

A repetition of these frightening experiences may trigger in the child a defensive exclusion of the information that ordinarily mobilizes help-seeking or attachment behavior. Children make themselves not notice that they need help because they know that help will not be forthcoming. This defensive exclusion deactivates the attachment system, with the result that the child's impulse to explore is not counterbalanced by the ability to keep track of when it is safe to explore and when it is safe to seek the parent's protection. This disruption of secure base behavior leads to unchecked exploration, as if the child is attempting to mobilize protective parental response by testing the limits of what is permissible. The counterphobic nature of reckless behavior lies in the child's implicit search for an answer to the questions: "Does my mother care enough for me that she will not let me get hurt? How much danger is so much that my mother will protect me? How far do I need to go before my mother will bring me back?"

Often, this behavior is labeled as "negative attention seeking" by parents and professionals who are not aware of young children's intense need to be loved and protected. An alternative explanation is that the child is attempting to gain mastery of overwhelming fear and helplessness by creating and recreating a frightening scenario in hopes of bringing about a happier resolution than before. As the pediatrician and child psychoanalyst Reginald Lourie put it: "Babies are very patient. They repeat something again and again until adults get it."

The goal of the intervention, in these cases, it to convey the message that the adults understand the urgency of the child's call for protection. Intervention strategies must show that the adults care about the child's safety and will not allow the child to be hurt. This message must establish, implicitly and explicitly, the adult's willingness and competence in taking care of the child. The adult must convey self-confidence in knowing better than the child which behaviors can be allowed and which behaviors are out of bounds for the sake of the child's well-being and the well-being of others. The hallmarks of interventions geared to containing and decreasing recklessness and self-endangerment are clear statements and actions that stop self-injurious behavior and speak to the importance of safety and protection. The clinician should consider an incremental approach in which the level of response is dictated by the degree and immediacy of danger and the appropriateness of the parent's response.

ITEMS AND CLINICAL EXAMPLES

1. **When the child behaves in a self-endangering way, the clinician brings the parent's attention to the risk and engages in a conversation about the importance of recognizing danger and offering protection and safety.**

   Example: Rowena, age 8 months, bangs her head repeatedly on the floor and against the wall. Her mother looks on but does nothing. The clinician asks what the mother thinks of that behavior. The mother replies: "It doesn't seem to hurt her. She's not crying." The clinician says: "Yes, but it worries me that she is not crying. It's like she is teaching herself not to feel pain." The mother says, with a little smile: "Like me." The clinician asks: "Do you want her to be like you in that way?" The mother thinks for a minute, looking at Rowena, who is continuing to bang her head. Without saying a word, she goes over to the child and picks her up. The clinician says: "You are showing her that she doesn't need to stop feeling, that you will help her when she needs you."

   Example: Andrew, age 3, runs down the sidewalk ahead of his mother and the clinician. In alarm, the clinician asks the mother: "Will he stop before he gets to the corner?" The mother yells out: "Andrew, stop right now." Andrew continues to run. The mother runs after Andrew and retrieves him, but says nothing to him. The clinician says: "Andrew, your mom and I were worried that a car could hit you. When she tells you to stop, you need to stop." She then says to the mother: "I guess he had no idea why you asked him to stop. He is so little that he does not yet know he can get hurt—he just likes to run."

In this example, the essential first intervention was to ask the mother whether the child would stop when he got to the corner. In a different case, with another 3-year-old, the child ran ahead of his mother and the therapist on the sidewalk. Again, the therapist asked the mother, "Will he stop before he gets to the corner?" The mother replied, "He will. He always does." She continued walking calmly. The therapist held her breath waiting to see what would happen. The child stopped, as his mother had predicted. If the therapist had run after the child it would have undermined his mother, implying that she could not read her child's responses or that she did not know to protect her child.

2. **When the parent seems at a loss about how to protect the child, the clinician actively guides the parent, using as specific and direct an approach as is required to elicit protective action.**

Example: Tamara, age 2, lets go of her mother's hand as they are crossing a busy street and runs ahead. There are no cars coming at the moment, but the clinician anticipates the possible danger and says to the mother: "Grab her quickly!" The mother runs after Tamara and takes her arm. Tamara yells "no!" and lets herself collapse on the crosswalk, refusing to hold her weight and walk. The mother keeps trying to pull her up, with no success. The clinician says: "I think you need to pick her up and carry her." The mother complies as Tamara cries bitterly but lets herself be carried. The clinician says to Tamara: "You are too little to cross the street by yourself. You always need to hold your mom's hand." As the critical moment subsides, the clinician asks the mother how she felt about the clinician telling her what to do, and asks if it is all right to do so again in the future if she realizes that the child is in danger.

3. **When the parent fails to take protective action that is urgently needed, the clinician models this behavior for the parent, enlisting the child's cooperation when feasible.**

Example: Andres, age 11 months, climbs on a table by an open window. Fearing that the child will fall, the clinician responds instantly and takes him down. He then says to the father: "I am sorry if I took over, I was too scared that he would fall." The father replies: "He wasn't going to fall." The clinician says: "Maybe you and I see danger differently. At this age they change so quickly that they can get hurt before you know it. What about if, just to be safe, we move the table away from the window?" The father agrees and he and the clinician move the table to the side.

Example: Danny, age 4, opens the door of the clinician's car when they arrive at their destination, and runs into the street. The clinician grabs him and says: "Damn it, Danny, you cannot do that. You can get hurt." Danny says, gleefully: "You said a bad word!" The clinician answers: "I did and I'm sorry, but this is really serious. You scared me a lot. I don't want you to ever do that again." The child replies: "Yes, ma'am." The clinician continues: "Now I want you to give your hand to your mom and to not let go until we tell you it is OK." The child says again, with utmost seriousness: "Yes, ma'am." The mother says, surprised: "He is really listening to you."

Domain V: Child Aggression Toward a Parent

Children who have witnessed their mother's battering often use physical or verbal aggression or both toward her in situations that elicit uncertainty, frustration, anger, or fear. This section focuses primarily on child aggression toward the mother because there are few clinical observations or empirical research involving children's aggression toward fathers. We have encountered occasional reports of children hitting their fathers to stop them from hitting their mothers, but we have not observed children being aggressive toward their fathers as a predictable or consistent interactional pattern. As more systematic child–father observation and intervention studies are conducted, a clearer picture of child aggression toward fathers in general and violent fathers in particular may emerge. By contrast, child aggression toward the mother is prevalent among the children we treat. For this reason, this section focuses on aggression toward the mother, and will be revised as more knowledge regarding aggression toward the father emerges.

Among children who have witnessed domestic violence, aggression toward the mother is a prevalent phenomenon. A variety of overlapping and mutually reinforcing mechanisms contribute to this aggressive response.

Different theoretical approaches conceptualize these mechanisms differently, but the underlying theme is that children incorporate into their behavioral repertoire aggressive actions that were witnessed in the course of family life. Possible mechanisms are outlined as follows:

- Children blame their mothers for the pain and difficulty of their lives. This includes believing that the mother is responsible for the separation from the father when the parents are not living together. For young children, the mother is an all-powerful figure who, in their minds, can do anything she wishes. They generalize her role as their primary caregiver into a belief that she can make things happen or not happen if only she wanted to. It follows that when faced with circumstances that sadden and anger them, they attribute their cause to the mother's power.

- The child might be reenacting aggressive scenes witnessed at home. Children imitate what they see, and are compelled to enact frightening and overwhelming experiences in an effort to understand what happened, elicit appropriate care from adults, and in this process master their feelings of helplessness and fear.

- The child might identify with the perpetrator of domestic violence against the mother and imitate his behavior, particularly if the perpetrator is also an attachment figure, such as the child's father or stepfather. Children strive to be like the people they love, and parents are particularly powerful role models that serve as a blueprint for children's behavior.

- Given that physical punishment is a socially prevalent form of discipline and that battered women tend to show increased harshness and punitiveness toward their children, the child might identify with and imitate the mother when engaging in aggression toward her.

- Children who have witnessed domestic violence tend to misperceive the intentions of others, overattributing hostile intent. This is particularly likely to occur when a parent is not only aggressive toward the spouse but also harsh and punitive in relation to the child. The child might then construct a perception of the parent as dangerous, frightening, and someone to be fought off for the purpose of self-protection. In these situations, child aggression toward the mother may be a mirror image of maternal aggression toward the child.

- Paradoxically, battered women may fail to protect themselves or to use appropriate limit setting when their children are physically or verbally aggressive toward them. They may give in to the child's demands in order to forestall the child's aggression. This maternal helplessness has the effect of confirming the child's perception that "aggression works," reinforcing aggressive action toward the mother. It is also possible that maternal helplessness, in itself, triggers child aggression because children equate helplessness with ineffectiveness in providing adequate care.

- Aggressive action is a frequent defensive response to intense fear and a profound sense of vulnerability. Children who have not been reliably protected by their attachment figures have not had opportunities to learn age-appropriate coping skills for managing intense negative emotions. As a result, their self-protective actions tend to be immediate and primitive, in the order of the biologically based "fight-or-flight" survival responses. Psychologically, it can be argued that aggression gives the child an in-the-moment feeling of mastery over overwhelming fear, which tends to perpetuate this response in children who are in a continuous state of exposure to frightening situations.

The clinician's response to the child's aggression toward the mother needs to take into account this variety of underlying mechanisms. **The main rationale for the intervention is to help the child acquire more appropriate modulation of negative feelings, including greater impulse control.** The goal is to help the child and the parent to stop or reduce their reliance on destructive and hurtful behaviors and to replace these behaviors with socially appropriate actions, including verbalization, alternative behaviors, and play.

In considering how to respond, the clinician needs to be attuned to the parents' feelings and perceptions of the child's behavior, and respectful of the family's cultural values and child-rearing mores. Parents may have strong reactions to the child's aggression, but they may not express these reactions in the presence of a nonfamily member, particularly someone whose opinion they value or who is perceived as having a position of power or authority, such as the clinician. The parent may feel humiliation, shame, anger, and a wish to retaliate, or may misperceive the child's aggression as humorous or loving. The therapist needs to be careful not to exacerbate the child–mother conflict or to embarrass the parents as a result of the intervention.

Witnessing aggression can generate a strong reaction in the clinician as well, setting the stage for a parallel process where unmodulated feelings in the family can lead to unmodulated feelings and impulsive action from the clinician. This is usually not helpful because the therapist's ability to contain intense negative reactions and to convey an attitude of calm and helpfulness are essential to the work. The clinician needs to keep a delicate balance between two polarities: impulsive action and passive observing. Impulsive action might come across as judgmental; doing nothing may indicate collusion with the aggression. Clinicians need to cultivate an inner stance where they train themselves to tolerate painful situations and give themselves permission to observe, but without becoming complacent in condoning hurtful actions. The clinician needs to feel free to take educated risks by intervening promptly, yet not feel forced to act before having a sense of what the appropriate intervention might be.

The items listed here intend to reflect this breadth of approach. The items are not mutually exclusive, but they comprise a range of complementary actions that can be used in conjunction with one another. In general, a "minimalist" approach to intervention is preferable because the goal of the intervention is to facilitate adaptive exchanges between parent and child rather than to have the clinician take center stage as the "expert." If the parent responds appropriately to the child, the intervention might consist of a simple show of understanding and "joining forces" with the parent (an exchange of knowing glances between clinician and parent might suffice). Failing this, the clinician encourages the parent to respond to the child. The therapist takes action only if the parent is unable or unwilling to do so, trying whenever possible to enhance the parent's sense of personal competence in the course of the intervention.

The "minimalist" philosophy extends to how to intervene with the child. Prevention is best, and consists of anticipating when the child is about to engage in an aggressive act. The clinician can then take action to distract the child and/or redirect the behavior.

The therapist can become the target of the child's aggression as well. The following items are easily adapted to allow the therapist to help the child in modulating, redirecting, or transforming this form of aggression.

Items and clinical examples

1. **The clinician encourages mother (and child, when age-appropriate) to think of behaviors that will allow the child to express anger in nonhurtful ways.**

Example: Nadia, 8 months, is teething. She constantly bites hard on anything that comes close, including her mother's face. The mother takes this personally, thinking that Nadia is hurting her on purpose. The clinician says: "I know it is hard not to take it personally, but let's observe Nadia together. She bites anything within reach, not just you." (The clinician shows the mother several examples). After the mother begins to realize the ubiquitousness of Nadia's biting, the clinician says: "Let's put together several things that Nadia can bite without hurting anybody. You can keep them at hand to give to her. But for the time being, be careful when you hold her close. She'll outgrow biting, but this is a time to be quicker than she is and to hold her at arm's length when you think she's ready to bite you." Mother and clinician assemble several cushiony objects that Nadia can chew on, and mother decides to buy a teething ring for good measure.

Example: Sonny, age 2, hits his mother when she tells him he needs to put the toys away. The mother turns to the clinician and says: "He always does that." The clinician says: "I think he is trying to tell you that he does not want to put the toys away, but for sure that is not the way to do it. How can he do it better?" The mother turns to Sonny and says: "You can tell me you are mad, but you can't hit me." Sonny says, "me mad, no hit," and then refuses to put the toys away. The clinician suggests he might need help to get going, and sets the example by putting one toy in the basket and saying: "See, Sonny, your mommy wants you to do what I do." A game ensues where mother, clinician, and child take turns in putting the toys in the basket.

2. **The therapist supports the mother's efforts to redirect the child's aggressive behavior, and uses age-appropriate language to explain that the mother is doing her job in teaching the child about right and wrong behavior.**

   Example: Tobias, 11 months, pinches his mother hard. The mother says: "No pinching, Tobias. Here, play with some modeling clay. That will keep your fingers busy." The clinician says: "Pinching modeling clay is OK, pinching Mommy is not OK."

Example: Sylvia, age 4, throws a block at her mother, barely missing the mother's face. The mother says: "Sylvia, you need to go to your room as punishment for trying to hurt me." The child screams, "I won't go. You go to your room." The mother tries to physically take Sylvia to her room, but the child runs away and taunts her mother to get her. The clinician says: "Sylvia, your mom is very serious. She really means it. She is your mommy and she is doing her job. You need to do what she says." The child goes to her room and in a few minutes announces from behind her closed door: "I am ready to come out now." The mother gives her permission to do so, and then says: "You need to apologize." The child says: "I am sorry." The clinician says: "Your mommy is teaching you not to do things that can hurt because that is scary for her and scary for you. I am here to help you with scary things like too much anger."

3. The therapist asks questions of the child and the mother that are aimed at understanding the meaning of the child's behavior for each of them.

Example: Sylvia, age 4, puts a pillow on her mother's face as the mother is reclining on the couch, holding it down tightly. The mother struggles to free herself. The clinician asks: "What just happened?" Sylvia answers: "My daddy did it." The mother explains that she and her husband used to have playful pillow fights that escalated into situations where he tried to suffocate her. The clinician says: "Sylvia, you are telling us that you remember what your daddy did when he lived with you." The child nods sadly. The clinician says: "It's hard to miss Daddy," and both mother and child nod their heads. (This exchange set the stage for further exchanges where the child's and the mother's conflicting feelings toward the father became recurrent themes, including their longing for the father, their fear of the father's unexpected swings from playfulness to anger, and their joint recreation of overexciting scenes where play and aggression mingled as a way of bringing the father back into their everyday life.)

4. When the child is verbally aggressive toward the parent (for example, by insulting or threatening the parent), the therapist acknowledges the

child's anger and states that this is not a good way of speaking to the mother.

> *Example*: Ruby, age 5, tells her mother: "You f— bitch." The clinician says: "I know you are angry, but that is not they way we do things around here."

5. The therapist creates an atmosphere where the meaning of behavior can be thought about and where different forms of behaving can be imagined and practiced. For this purpose, the clinician guides the mother and the child into a conversation about the child's aggression, the circumstances that triggered it, and the feelings that accompany it. This conversation might start with the clinician asking the parent what she thinks of the child's behavior. It is often useful to comment that the clinician finds it hard to see the child mistreating the mother, in order to make clear that aggressive behavior need not be accepted as a regular part of relationships.

> *Example*: In the previous example, the therapist follows up by saying to the mother: "How come Ruby is speaking that way to you?" The mother says she doesn't know. The therapist asks whether Ruby always does that, or whether anything happened that made her more upset that usual. The mother then reveals that Ruby had been with her father the day before, and soon afterward he had been taken to jail. Ruby had overheard the mother telling a friend that the father was in jail, and Ruby had been so upset that she had cried non-stop at school and had to be sent home. The therapist speaks sympathetically about this incident, and tells Ruby that maybe she is worried about her father. She then adds that sometimes when we are too worried we get angry more easily. At the end of the session, the therapist suggests to the mother that she might keep track of Ruby's behavior in the days that follow, because the child may well be more irritable and aggressive as a result of her worries about her father.

6. When immediate protective action seems necessary because the mother passively accepts the child's physical aggression, the clinician stops and redirects the child's behavior, first asking the parent for permission to do so, if feasible.

Example: Angela, 15 months, starts having a tantrum where she hits her mother repeatedly and screams when her mother takes the scissors away from her. The mother does not respond. The therapist asks the mother if it's OK if she steps in, and when the mother agrees she tells Angela: "You can hit this cushion, but you can't hit your mommy." Angela lifts her arm to hit the mother again; the therapist takes Angela's arm and redirects it, helping her hit the cushion. She says: "Hit the cushion, not Mommy. Mommy can't give you the scissors because you can get hurt." She holds Angela's hand, helping her hit the cushion several times, saying: "Hit the cushion, not Mommy," again and again.

There is some risk in trying this kind of intervention, and the therapist should know the child well before she does so. In our experience, many children become more and more agitated if they are encouraged to hit anything, even a pillow. Containing and calming the child may work more effectively for most children than allowing them to hit an object.

Example: Samuel, age 3, kicks the door angrily. Just as he gets ready to kick it again, the therapist says: "I bet you can stop." Surprised, Samuel stops briefly and looks at the therapist, who quickly says: "You stopped, Samuel! Good for you! Give me five!" Samuel smiles broadly and "gives five" to the clinician, who says, enthusiastically: "I knew you could stop, Samuel!" Samuel says: "I am a good boy." The mother and the therapist agree.

Example: Sylvia, age 4, takes a sharp object and yells: "I will poke your eyes out, Mommy" while waving it very close to her mother's face. The mother says weakly: "Don't do that," but the child escalates her behavior. The clinician says to the mother: "Do you mind if I speak with Sylvia?" The mother nods her head helplessly. The clinician approaches Sylvia and says firmly: "Put that down, Sylvia. You have to listen to your mother." Sylvia obeys. The clinician then says: "I know you are angry with your mommy, but you can't hurt her. It is not good for her and it is not good for you."

7. **If the mother misperceives the child's aggression as loving or playful behavior, the therapist expresses his or her point of view. If the mother**

insists the child was being loving or playful, the therapist suggests that this can become a topic for further exchanges.

Example: Lorraine, age 14 months, alternates between kissing her mother, licking her face, and biting her. The mother grimaces in pain, but lets the child continue doing it. The clinician asks: "How come you let her bite you?" The mother says: "She doesn't know she is hurting me." The clinician says: "You might be right, but I think she is experimenting to see if it hurts you or not, and she needs to learn that it does." The mother says: "I don't want her to feel guilty." The clinician replies: "But how will she learn not to hurt you unless you teach her?" The mother says: "She's too little right now. She'll learn in time." The clinician answers: "It's hard for me to watch when you are hurt, but I guess we can continue talking about it." The mother says: "Don't worry, it doesn't hurt that much." The clinician says, lightly: "You have to forgive me, but it's hard for me to believe that." The topic switches as the mother puts Lorraine down and gives her a toy.

Example: Reuben, age 4, responds to a maternal command by jumping up, pointing her finger at her as if it were a gun, and saying: "Don't make me have to shoot you, mommy." The mother laughs. The therapist asks what she finds funny, and the mother responds that he looks just like a cowboy, very cute. The therapist says, "I find him very cute most of the time, but not when he wants to shoot you." The mother shrugs her shoulders and answers: "He is just playing. Children play." The clinician says: "You know, I think he was kind of serious about it. You and I are seeing it differently. Maybe we can think about it some more as we continue to meet." In a later session, the mother remarks that Reuben is having trouble at school because he hits, and again she laughs as she tells the story. Reuben laughs too. The therapist comments on this, and the mother says: "He is so cute when he gets angry, but I know it can get him in trouble." The clinician says: "I think he likes it when you find him cute, and maybe that makes him hit more." Mother is silent. Turning to Reuben, the clinician says: "Your mom and I are talking about hitting. We are trying to think of ways of helping you not to hit."

8. **When the child's aggression is a response to the mother's harshness, the clinician speaks to the anger between them and introduces the theme of finding nonhurtful ways of expressing anger.**

> *Example:* Camilo, age 4, kicks his mother in the leg after she pulls his ear in punishment because he did not obey her harsh command to turn off the TV. The mother says, in exasperation: "You are bad! You are just like your father!" The clinician says: "Could we take a look at what just happened?" There is a silence. The clinician asks: "Camilo, can you tell us why you kicked your mother?" Camilo says, very clearly, looking at his mother: "You are mean." The mother lifts her eyes to the ceiling, as if asking the Heavens for mercy. The clinician says: "She's mean? How is she mean?" Camilo says: "She hurt my ear." The clinician says: "She hurt your ear, and then you kicked her because you were angry?" Camilo nods. The clinician turns to the mother and asks: "What do you think?" The mother says: "I need to teach him to obey. He never does what I tell him to do." The clinician says: "You get angry at Camilo and hurt him and then Camilo gets angry at you and hurts you." There is a silence. The clinician asks: "Is there a way that you won't need to hurt each other?" Camilo says to his mother: "I want you to speak to me like this: 'My dear little Camilo, can you please turn off the TV?'" The mother bursts out laughing, joined by the clinician and, after a brief delay, by Camilo. The clinician says: "You want your mom to be very polite with you," and Camilo nods. The clinician says: "I know what you mean. It's nice when people speak nicely to us." The mother says to the clinician: "I don't know where he learns these things." The clinician replies: "I have seen you speak very nicely to him. I think he likes it so much he wishes you were always that way with him." The mother looks pensive. She then says to her son: "I am not a very polite person, Camilo. But I won't pull your ear and I don't want you to kick me."

9. **When the mother is so angry at the child's aggression that she is unable to perceive the child's appropriate remorse, the therapist calls her attention to it while supporting the legitimacy of her feelings.**

Example: The mother of Mandy, age 4, reports angrily that Mandy punched her in the stomach earlier in the day and that it hurt very much. As she starts speaking, Mandy leans against her and hides his face in the mother's chest. The clinician asks what happened, and the mother reports that, while the movers were in the apartment, taking the belongings of a roommate who was moving out, Mandy came "out of the blue" and punched her very hard. Mandy's face was still buried in the mother's chest. The clinician says: "You know, I'm sure Mandy's punch really did hurt because he is a strong boy. And, I think that for Mandy, having all these people here this morning, and knowing that your roommate that he likes is moving out, and everybody talking excitedly and things being moved out of the apartment, all that was sad and confusing. Sometimes when you're small you can feel lost and unseen and not be able to control how you get your mommy's attention, but I can see that Mandy seems upset that he hurt you." The mother's tone of voice becomes much warmer as she comments: "Well, Mommy doesn't like it when Mandy hits her and we will have to try really hard not to let it happen again." Mandy lifts his head from the mother's chest and motions that he wants to whisper something in her ear. Mandy gently moves the mother's hair from her ear and whispers: "Can we play with the doll house now?" The mother responds: "Yes, now we can play with the doll house."

10. **When the child's aggression indicates a misunderstanding of the parent's motives, the therapist explains what is happening in order to help the child achieve a more accurate perception of reality. This may involve bringing in other relevant themes in the child's life that fuel the child's distorted perception of the parent's intentions.**

Example: The mother of Carina, age 4, reports in a very upset tone of voice that the child hit her and told her to "go away" at a party. The clinician turns to Carina and repeats what the mother said in a surprised tone of voice. The mother starts crying, and the child brings her some tissue. The clinician comments that the mother could probably use some because she seems very sad. The child goes back to playing with the dollhouse, with her back to the mother. The mother says that Carina had gotten very angry at her at the party because there was no pineapple pizza, which is her favorite kind of pizza. With much feeling, the therapist says to Carina: "Oooh, you must have been very angry." Carina nods. The therapist adds: "I bet you thought it was your mom's fault that there was no pineapple pizza." Carina nods but remains turned to the doll house. The mother's face brightens with a new understanding. The therapist continues: "Well, sometimes when we are 4 years old, we think our mommies are so big and strong that they can get anything we want. Like they can make pineapple pizza come and they can even make our daddy come when we want him. And the mommy really wants to help and even asks the aunt to order pineapple pizza or asks the daddy to come visit, and no matter how hard the mommy tries, things just don't happen. And then the mommy's feelings get hurt when she tries so hard and still the little girl is angry because she couldn't make it happen." Carina turns around and jumps on her mother's arms, hugging her tightly.

Domain VI: Child Aggression Toward Peers, Siblings, or Others

There is substantial research evidence that children exposed to marital conflict and violence have problems in peer relationships. These problems may be manifested in aggression toward peers or in being bullied by them. Such findings are expectable in light of the increased incidence of clinically significant problem behaviors in these children when compared to non-exposed peers. Many of the causal mechanisms implicated in aggression toward the mother are at work in triggering children's aggression to peers as well. Common factors are anxious attachment, the lack of adaptive social skills and coping mechanisms to handle frustration, and the tendency to misinterpret neutral social cues, to overreact, and to strike back in response to peer rejection. Although research on sibling aggression in the first 5 years is limited, there is abundant clinical evidence indicating that siblings, particularly younger ones, are the most likely peers to become the brunt of children's aggression because of daily, moment-to-moment proximity and the competition for scarce resources, particularly the parent's attention and love.

The opportunities for direct intervention with peer aggression are necessarily limited in a therapeutic setting because peers are not present, but children and mothers often report on the child's difficulties in the child-care or preschool setting, and these reports provide an entry point for intervention. More direct intervention is possible in sibling conflicts when treatment is conducted in the home. Although the primary focus of child–parent psychotherapy is the attachment relationship, this focus is defined broadly because the attachment relationship is deeply affected by the children's perception of how they fit in the emotional landscape of the household. Sibling rivalry is fueled by the child's fear that the parent prefers one child to the others. The overall treatment goal of adaptive affect modulation and expression must include the child's ability to develop reciprocal and loving relationships with siblings and peers and to negotiate conflict with them in nonhurtful ways. Intervention strategies need to take into account that self-endangering behavior, aggression toward the mother, and aggression toward others (including the clinician) can occur in quick succession because the child's anger, when blocked, can turn from one target to another, becoming diffuse and uncontrolled.

ITEMS AND CLINICAL EXAMPLES

1. **When the child or the parent report that the child used physical aggression against a peer, the clinician starts a calm discussion of the event, including an understanding of how it came about, the meaning of the child's behavior, and alternative ways of expressing anger.**

   Example: The mother of Yael, age 5, reports that in preschool that morning the child had pushed her friend Paula when Paula's father arrived to pick her up. The mother had witnessed the episode and called out to Yael, but the child did not respond. A teacher then told the mother that Yael always hits or pushes Paula when Paula's father comes to take his daughter home. The clinician now asks Yael what happened that made her push Paula when Paula's father arrived. Yael explains that she likes Paula's father and that she wanted to go home with him, but she couldn't. The clinician asks: "Does that make you sad and also angry?" Yael responds: "I get sad." The clinician asks if Yael wants a father like Paula's father. Yael says: "I have my grandpa but he lives far away and I don't see him." The clinician comments that Yael is sad because she misses her grandfather. Yael says: "I was good in school today and I will go to kindergarten." The clinician replies: "I know you want to be good, but you pushed Paula, and I think you are worried that the teacher will not let you go to kindergarten." Yael says: "The teacher says I can't hit if I want to go to kindergarten." The clinician says: "Let's think of what else you can do instead of pushing or hitting Paula.... Can you go to a quiet place and say to yourself: 'I am sad and angry because I am not going home with Paula and her father, but I can't push her and I can't hit her because I want to go to kindergarten'?" Yael says: "Yeah."

2. **When the child's aggression toward others seems related to parental physical aggression toward the child, the therapist helps the parent see the connection between the two and encourages a change in the parent's as well as the child's behavior.**

> *Example:* The mother of Linda, age 4, and Sandy, age 2, reports that the children are hitting other children at school when they do not get their way. Sandy also hit a teacher that morning. The therapist asks if anything happened in the family to make Sandy hit the teacher, and the mother shrugs her shoulders, saying that everything is the same and that she is baffled by this sudden aggression. The therapist asks if it was really sudden, and the mother admits that Sandy's behavior has been slowly getting worse over time. The therapist asks the mother to describe a couple of recent times when she got upset with the children. The mother readily describes several incidents when she immediately yelled: "Stop it!" and slapped them. The mother adds, spontaneously, as an afterthought: "I guess they are doing what I do." The therapist asks how she feels about it, and the mother says: "I really don't know any other way of doing it; it's an automatic response." The therapist suggests that one way of making it less automatic is to start paying close attention to her feelings as they build up, so she can do something before getting so angry that she snaps. The mother remembers an occasion when the therapist helped her talk about her feelings about a frustrating situation; she felt better afterward even though the situation had not changed. The therapist says: "I remember that. Do you think it can also work if you use that with your children?" The mother says: "Well, when Linda looks at me with those 'don't mess with me' eyes I feel like clobbering her. Maybe I can stop myself if I

try." The therapist turns to the children and says: "Your mommy and I are talking about how all of you are going to try not to hit." As mother and children are leaving the playroom at the end of the session, there is an opportunity to practice this because Linda grabs something from Sandy's hand and Sandy lifts her hand to hit her. Before she can do it, the mother grabs Sandy's hand, and then turns uncertainly toward the therapist, who steps in to help, saying: "Linda and Sandy, your mommy really means it that she doesn't want to slap you any more, and she doesn't want you to slap each other. You need to tell each other in words what you want." A conversation ensues about what triggered the conflict and how to solve it, with the therapist guiding the mother in this effort.

3. **When the child engages in aggressive behavior, the clinician tries to set up a situation that deescalates the behavior.**

   Example: Paulo, age 4, is swinging a yo-yo in a way that can hit his older brother. The mother has gone momentarily out of the room. The clinician tells the older brother to move away from Paulo so that he will not get hit. The brother complies. The clinician then says to Paulo: "Paulo, we can't be close to you when you are doing something that can hurt us. You have to stop doing that." Paulo responds by making smaller circles as he continues to wave the yo-yo. The clinician says: "That is better, but it is still not good enough. Make the circles even smaller." Paulo complies. The circles are now so small that they pose no danger to a bystander. The clinician says: "Good job, Paulo. Now it is safe to be near you." Paulo looks visibly pleased. He stops swinging the yo-yo and tries to make it go up and down.

4. **When the child engages in escalating aggressive behavior, the therapist takes whatever steps are needed to ensure safety until the aggressive behavior subsides, assuring the child that the adults will take care of him and not let him hurt himself or others.**

   Example: Danny, age 4, is pushing the swing in a way that is threatening to hit his sister Dottie, who is toddling about. The clinician suggests a game that he likes, but he looks at her defiantly and keeps moving the swing in his sister's direction. The mother tries to take his hand to bring him over, but he suddenly starts writhing and kicking at her. Seeing that she seems scared and helpless, the clinician goes over to help restrain him, but the child seems stronger than both adults. The clinician instructs the mother that they will divide their efforts, and both hold him to stop him from kicking. The mother holds Danny's legs and the clinician holds his upper body. He flails and writhes very hard, and both have to struggle very hard to stop him from hitting and kicking them. He starts screaming: "I want to kill myself! Kill me, kill me! You don't love me!," looking at his mother. He then looks at the clinician, and screams: "Don't touch me!" The clinician tells him that she and his mother are holding him because first he was trying to hurt his sister and then his mother and now he was saying that he wanted to hurt himself, and his mother and the clinician did not want that to happen. In all of this, as soon as he was able to free one arm, he would hit his mother or punch his own face. He also managed to bite his mother's hands. He also kept screaming that his mother did not love him. She would say, tentatively: "You know that I love you very much?" He would wail: "No, you don't love me!" The clinician tells him that both of his parents loved him and wanted him to be safe, but sometimes they did not know how to show it. He wails that this is not true, and screams to the mother: "You call me stupid!" The mother freezes, and the clinician speaks for her, saying that his mother is sorry that she called him names, and then asks the mother to tell him the same thing. All along, the clinician has been talking to the mother, saying things like: "You are doing really well, it is hard to hold him," and "He is very scared and wants us to reassure him that we won't let him hurt himself and that is why we have to keep him still." The clinician now says to the mother: "Tell him that you want to keep him safe." The mother hesitates, and the clinician says more firmly that he needs to hear her say it. She says it, half-heartedly. The clinician encourages the mother to tell him that she loves him and would try not to call him names. She says, in a questioning tone: "You know I love you?" Danny yells:

"No!!!" The clinician tells the mother to keep it simple, saying only: "I love you. I will keep you safe." The mother repeats these words several times, with increasing conviction, and then she begins to hold Danny more effectively.

Danny then starts asking the clinician to let go of him. The clinician answers that she does not want to let go of him because earlier he hit his mom and himself when he had his arms free. She says that she will let go of one of his hands and see whether he is more calm, adding: "If I see that you won't hit yourself or your mom when I let go of one hand, then I will let go of you." She lets go of his hand, and the child does not hit. The clinician says to the mother: "Let's let go of him and see if he is calm." They both let go of him, and he cradles up in his mother's lap very quietly, leaning against her. The mother puts her arms tightly around him, and he almost immediately falls asleep.

Domain VII: Parental Use of Physical Punishment

The use of physical punishment as a form of child discipline is a source of heated controversy. It is widely used in the United States, but it is met with almost uniform disapproval by child development professionals. Social class and cultural factors play an important role in how people perceive the use of physical punishment. When there is a social class difference between parent and clinician, the implicit power differential between both parties can become more acute when the clinician expresses disapproval of the parental actions. Similarly, when the clinician and the parent belong to different cultural (i.e., ethnic or national) backgrounds, it is easy for parents to feel that the clinician is expressing disapproval for their traditional patterns of child rearing. Recent immigrants who are unfamiliar with the range of child-rearing mores in the United States might be particularly vulnerable to feelings of insecurity and defensiveness, whereas ethnic minorities with histories of discrimination may react with anger and resentment at perceived efforts to impose child-rearing patterns that feel alien to them.

Physical punishment takes a variety of forms, from a mild slap on the child's hand or bottom to slapping the child's face, pulling hair, pinching, biting, using an object to inflict pain, and leaving marks on the child's body. We take the position that, although an occasional mild slap on the hand or bottom is not likely to have a serious deleterious effect on the child, it is not an optimal form of discipline and it should be discouraged. This is particularly the case for children who have witnessed violence, and who as a result tend to be hypervigilant and hyper-responsive to threats and danger signals that would seem minor to other children. For this reason, we recommend that any form of physical punishment needs to be addressed with the parent at some point, not necessarily in the moment but at a time when there can be constructive discussion. The clinician should always make an explicit effort to understand and respect the cultural underpinnings of the parent's use of physical punishment, even when disagreeing with it.

Few situations arouse as strong a feeling of disapproval toward parents as watching them be harshly physically punitive to their children. The clinician must develop a deep conviction that, although parental physical punishment is inappropriate, it does not justify becoming judgmental or punitive toward the parent. One must avoid enacting a parallel process by which the clinician becomes harsh with the parent who is harsh with the child. The goal of the intervention is not to give the parent moral instruction but to enable to parent to have better impulse control and to modulate strong negative feelings, including anger and fear. For this goal to be met, clinicians must have the capacity to restrain their own punitive impulses toward the parent and to modulate their anger and disapproval of the way the child is being treated. Remembering that punitiveness toward the child is rooted in the parents' own experiences of harsh and inappropriate punishment often helps the clinician to curb angry and critical feelings. It is also important to remember that, whenever possible, discipline needs to be discussed as an effort to help the child learn rather than as a form of punishment.

There is sometimes disagreement among professionals and even among child welfare workers about which kinds of physical punishment qualify as legally reportable physical abuse. When the clinician is in doubt, we recommend calling the Child Protective Services Emergency Response Unit to describe the incident and ask for advice. This section of the manual focuses on forms of physical punishment that do not qualify as child abuse. The next section focuses on procedures to follow for reporting possible child abuse.

<u>Items and clinical examples</u>

1. **When the parent uses socially accepted physical punishment (e.g., a mild slap on the child's hand or buttocks), the clinician finds an appro-**

priate time, preferably after the heat of the moment has subsided, to ask the parent about her values and beliefs about how children should be disciplined. This opportunity is used to develop a dialogue about this topic, to offer developmental guidance if the parent seems receptive to it, or to discuss how the parent was brought up if this seems appropriate.

Example: Briana, age 4 months, kicks vigorously while her mother is changing her diapers. Mother slaps her on the bottom, not too hard but firmly. Briana startles and stops moving, making a brief noise of distress. The clinician asks if it bothers her when Briana is so active. The mother says: "Yes, she doesn't like to be changed and she's making it hard for me to do it." The clinician asks: "What do you hope she'll learn when you slap her?" The mother answers: "To stop moving and cooperate." The clinician says: "I think she had no idea that is what you want. She looked so surprised. I think she was just so happy to be out of those soiled diapers and was letting you know how good it felt to be free." The mother looks skeptical but listens attentively.

Example: Mario, age 2, pulls his baby brother's hair. His mother slaps him on the hand. Both Mario and his brother cry. The mother picks up the wailing baby and consoles him, while Mario sobs loudly alone in a corner. The clinician looks at the mother sympathetically and says: "I guess everybody is having a hard time." The mother looks overwhelmed, and the clinician asks if she can talk to Mario while the mother consoles the baby. The mother agrees, and the clinician speaks softly to Mario, telling him that she knows it is very hard to be hit and to watch his mother hold his baby brother instead of him. When things calm down, the clinician asks the mother whether she finds that slapping works as a way of teaching Mario how to behave. The mother says, ruefully: "It hasn't worked yet, but I hope some day it will." The clinician asks if that is the way she was disciplined while growing up, and the mother replies that it was. The clinician asks: "What was it like for you? Do you feel it was useful as you grew up?" The mother says: "It taught me respect. I was afraid of my parents, but I respected them." The clinician asks: "Is that how you want Mario to feel about you?" The mother says: "I want him to respect me, but I don't want him to be afraid of me." The clinician answers: "I can understand that, and there are ways of doing it. Children Mario's age really want to please their parents, even if sometimes it is hard to believe that they do. They love it when their parents approve of them, and they feel bad when the parents disapprove of what they do. If you tell Mario what you like and what you don't like, I think he will learn it very well. If you like, next time Mario does something wrong when I am here, we can try it together and see how it works."

3. **The clinician asks the parent for her motivation in using physical punishment, asks the child how she or he felt, and guides parent and child toward a dialogue about how each of them sees the situation that led to physical punishment.**

Example: Lisa's mother slaps her on the bottom when the child uses a dirty word to refer to her sister. Lisa, age 4, looks at her mother with angry eyes but says nothing. The mother tells her angrily: "I can hit you again just for giving me that look." Turning to the clinician, she says: "I hate that look. It is so hateful." The clinician asks the mother what she wanted to show Lisa when she slapped her. The mother says: "I want her to learn not to use dirty words." The clinician says to Lisa: "What do you think about that, Lisa?" Lisa replies: "She says the same word to me." The mother protests that Lisa is lying. The clinician says: "You want to use the same words that your mom uses, and you get angry when she punishes you for it?" Lisa says "Yes." The mother says: "Maybe sometimes I use that word, but I'm a grown-up and you are a child." The clinician says: "I see your point, but I bet Lisa doesn't. She thinks you're cool, and she wants to be like you."

4. **The clinician finds an appropriate time to suggest an alternative to physical punishment that teaches the child about unwanted consequences for undesirable behavior.**

Example: Joe, age 3, is climbing on his mother's dresser and falls, banging his head on the floor and nearly pulling the dresser over on top of him. His mother runs to him and pulls him away. Mother and child are clearly frightened. The mother checks Joe's

head and is able to calm him in a few minutes. After he stops crying, she says: "I have to get the paddle now." Joe jumps, runs away
from her with a terrorized look, and stands mutely in the corner
of the room, shaking. The clinician says to the mother: "Could we
please talk about it for a minute? Joe looks so frightened. Can we
see if there is anything else that can teach him without frightening him so much?" The mother stops but replies he deserves the
paddle. The clinician says: "Look at him. He just fell and hurt his
head. Do you think maybe that is what he should learn, that if he
climbs on the dresser something bad will happen? Isn't falling
and hurting his head the lesson that he needs to learn?" The
mother relents, and says to Joe: "OK, no paddling for today, but
don't you ever climb on that dresser again." During this conversation, Joe continues to tremble and to stare at his mother with a
frozen gaze. He gradually relaxes after she tells him that she will
not paddle him.

5. **When the parent expresses a religious or cultural conviction that physical punishment is morally necessary, the clinician explains that children
who witnessed violence, particularly involving loved ones, are emotionally overwhelmed by physical punishment and unable to learn from it.**

> *Example*: Sam, age 3, drops a glass on the floor as he reaches
> across the table to retrieve a toy. The glass breaks. His mother
> yells at him and slaps him on the bottom. Sam cries heartily while
> the mother berates him for the mess he made. The clinician lis-
> tens and observes quietly. She then helps the mother to pick up
> the pieces of glass and mop up the spilled water. When the mood
> softens, the clinician asks: "Do you usually slap Sam when he
> does something wrong?" The mother says she does. The clinician
> asks: "How did you decide to do that?" The mother says: "I am a
> Christian, and in the Bible it says that if you spare the rod you
> spoil the child." The clinician comments: "I can see that your reli-
> gion is very important to you." The mother replies: "It certainly is.
> I go to church three times a week, and my pastor is very helpful
> to me." The clinician asks in what ways her pastor is helpful. The
> mother answers: "I am a single mother, my child has no father.
> My pastor is like a father to him. He helps me when I don't know
> what to do with Sam." The clinician asks if the pastor believes that

sparing the rod spoils the child. The mother says with conviction: "He sure does. He taught me that." The clinician says: "You know, I respect how important it is for you to learn from your pastor what it says in the Bible. Let me tell you what I am thinking. Maybe you can ask your pastor about it. He certainly knows the Bible much better than I do, and I wouldn't want to tell you anything that goes against your religion. But one thing that we learned about children who saw a lot of violence between their mother and father is that hitting is not helpful in teaching them how to behave. It reminds them of how scared they got when their mom and dad fought, and they get so scared all over again that they can't learn what you are trying to teach them. What they actually learn is that hitting is OK, and they start hitting also because it makes them feel less scared, like they are strong and able to defend themselves. I worry that if you slap Sam as a way of teaching him, then he will start slapping because he'll think that if you do it, then it means it's fine for him to do it too." The mother says: "I never thought about it that way. I will tell my pastor what you are saying and ask him what he thinks about it." (In a subsequent session, the mother reported that her pastor agreed with the clinician's recommendation, and she decided to stop hitting the child.)

6. **When the clinician believes that discussing the parent's use of physical punishment in front of the child would be perceived as disrespectful by the parent, the clinician waits for a private moment to raise the topic or requests a telephone appointment or an individual session with the parent.**

Example: The mother of Khalil, age 4, slaps him on the hand for wanting to drink from her glass. "It is my juice. Go get yourself some of your own," she says. Khalil complies. Knowing that the mother has strong feelings about being in charge of Khalil, the clinician takes advantage of his being in the kitchen to say: "You know, I think that Khalil's hitting at school might have something to do with what happened just now. Could I come a little earlier next time, so we can talk about it before Khalil is back from school?" The mother says: "I'm not too sure what you're getting at, but sure." The conversation stops when Khalil returns from the kitchen with a glass of juice and offers some to the clinician.

7. **If it becomes clear that the parent and clinician have widely divergent views and values about the use of physical punishment, the clinician acknowledges that this is the case, and suggests an ongoing discussion of this topic to see if areas of agreement could emerge.**

> *Example:* Amelia, age 15 months, spills juice on the carpet, and her mother matter-of-factly slaps her on the hand. Amelia does not respond. The clinician comments that Amelia seems to take the slap in stride. The mother says: "She's used to it. She knows that I slap her when she does something wrong." The clinician asks if slapping helps Amelia not do things wrong. The mother says: "Of course. If I slap her, she knows she is not supposed to do it again." The clinician says: "I actually think that sometimes children get confused. Maybe they know they did something wrong, but they don't know how to make it right." The mother says, forcefully: "Of course they know. Like now, Amelia knows she needs to be more careful with her juice. Don't you, Amelia?" Amelia nods soberly. The mother says to the clinician: "See? I told you. She knows." The clinician says: "I guess this is one place where we see things differently. I think Amelia is trying very hard to please you, but she doesn't know how to be more careful with the juice. Let's continue talking about it in the future and see whether we can understand where each of us is coming from." The mother says: "That's OK by me."

8. **When the clinician finds himself or herself flooded with strong feelings of anger and disapproval toward the parent, he or she refrains from taking immediate action and engages in an internal process of searching for emotional balance and modulation of feelings.**

> *Example:* Charlie, age 30 months, does not respond fast enough when his mother asks him to bring her something from the kitchen, and she slaps him quite hard while telling him angrily that he never listens and he is trying to annoy her on purpose. While Charlie cries, the mother tells him that he is just pretending to be scared and that he is a manipulator. The clinician feels

flooded by rage at the mother, with whom she has been working for many months to help her understand that toddlers do not always respond readily to commands. The clinician feels a strong desire to yell at the mother that she is mean and nasty and that the clinician is sick and tired of working with her. The clinician has a clear internal image of herself walking out the door while calling the mother names. As she is struggling with these feelings, the mother expresses regret for having hit Charlie and apologizes to the child. The clinician remains internally very angry and imagines herself telling the mother that her regret comes too late and that she is a terrible mother. At the same time, the clinician keeps telling herself: "You know that there is more here than meets the eye. Think. Think. Try to understand why she is acting this way in front of you." After about 2 minutes, the clinician remembers the mother's abysmal sense that she is no good and that she deserves nothing good, a theme the mother has often spoken about in previous sessions. She says to the mother: "There are times when it is hard to remember how patient you can be with Charlie because the anger is so hot and so real, and when that happens you get really down on yourself. But it is important for us to remember that you can come back to the part of you that does not want to hurt Charlie, and to keep reminding Charlie of that so he does not forget." Turning to Charlie, she says: "Your mom is trying really hard to learn not to hit, but sometimes it takes a long time to learn." Charlie nods his head sadly, as if saying he understood. The mother's eyes fill with tears, and she says softly: "I wish it did not take so long, honey."

9. **When the parent is unresponsive to other forms of intervention, the clinician urges the parent, politely but firmly, not to hit or use physical punishment because it is not good for the child's respect for the parent and healthy development.**

Example: The mother is describing in exacting detail, clearly quite satisfied with herself, how she "whooped" her child for being sassy. The clinician listens, fully aware that he has tried many tactful forms of intervention before, all to no avail. He feels that he has a good relationship with the mother, who trusts his good judgement without necessarily always following his advice.

The child is out of hearing in the next room, and the clinician feels that he can disagree with the mother without humiliating her in front of the child. He says: "Adela, I know we have talked about this before, but I really need to tell you something. You need to find other ways of teaching Monique not to be sassy. Hitting her is no good. She will think that she is no good, and she will also lose respect for you." The mother laughs heartily, and says: "If I do what you say, will you come and keep her in line when she is a teenager?" The clinician says, also laughingly: "You will need me more if you keep hitting her. She will become a wild teenager, and then how will you stop her? She could even hit you back because she will be stronger and quicker than you! We need to find ways of teaching her that you can use even when she is a teenager."

Domain VIII: Parental Use of Derogatory Names, Threats, or Criticism of the Child

Parents can cause considerable emotional damage by calling their children by derogatory names, ridiculing them, being harshly critical, and threatening them. These parental behaviors present a difficult therapeutic challenge. Clinicians do not want to appear as if they are criticizing the parent or taking the child's side, yet continued failure to act can have the effect of colluding with the parent, confirming the supposed "truth" of the criticism or the rightness of the threat, and leaving the child emotionally alone.

Optimally, the clinician's response needs to simultaneously express interest and empathy for the parent's anger and frustration, and empathic support for the child's fear and worry in response to the parent. The overall attitude to be conveyed is a wish to create a more positive emotional climate between parent and child. For this to happen, the clinician's emotional position needs to be equidistant between parent and child. Compassion for the child's suffering must be balanced by awareness that the parent also suffers, although this pain is covered over by anger and bitterness.

It helps to remember that the focus of the intervention is neither the parent nor the child as individuals, but rather their relationship. When witnessing a difficult scene between parent and child, clinicians need to give themselves permission to do nothing if they find themselves in an internal state of turmoil and confusion. Although complacency should be discouraged, it is better to do nothing temporarily than to intervene out of anger, striking out blindly at the parent in a futile effort to protect the child.

Knowing about events that happened during the week or prior to the session is often essential for constructive intervention. Behaviors that seem inexplicable or irrational suddenly acquire clear meaning when one knows about real life events or about how a person has been feeling. Asking direct questions about what happened since the last session can provide a context that clarifies the reasons for the parent's anger or the child's defiant, sullen, aggressive, or recalcitrant behavior.

The items that follow involve interventions that often overlap with each other. In the flow of the session, clinicians often start with one strategy that is followed and complemented by another. Interventions are not "sound bites," but part of a concerted effort to enhance intimacy and communication between parent and child, help them express intense feelings in nonfrightening ways, and help them modulate and regulate overwhelming emotion. An overarching goal of all the intervention strategies suggested is to develop a joint plan for appropriate alternative behaviors. Clearly, this goal cannot be achieved in every session or as a result of every intervention. However, the clinician needs to take every opportunity to help the parent and the child develop and practice specific forms of behavior that feel safer as well as more comforting and pleasurable.

ITEMS AND CLINICAL EXAMPLES

1. **When the parent is harshly critical of the child, the clinician first empathizes with the anger and frustration whenever possible, and then explores why the child's behavior prompted this response. In this process, the clinician offers alternative explanations that give a different and more balanced meaning to the child's behavior. These suggestions may involve reframing the child's behavior or the parent's perception of it, suggesting possible motives for the child's behavior that the parent might be unaware of, and/or describing the developmental appropriateness of the child's reaction.**

   Example: Lisa and her mother are talking about the mother's boyfriend leaving without saying good-bye. The mother is saying that she has been depressed all week, barely able to make herself go to work and grouchy and exhausted when she gets home. Lisa, age 4, is looking very sad. The mother notices it and starts rubbing Lisa's back. Lisa comes closer to the mother, falling back so that the mother can do it more easily. The mother then starts playing with the toy dishes, trying to engage Lisa. She tickles Lisa and hands her a plate of pretend food, but the child refuses to take it. Lisa starts to whine and sort of commands her mother to continue rubbing her back. The mother's empathic mood changes abruptly, and she yells: "Don't whine. Use your words. I don't want to rub you any more. Let's play." Lisa starts crying loudly. The mother turns to the clinician and says angrily: "You see, she never gets enough. She always wants more." Turning back to Lisa, she says: "I rubbed your back for a long time, and I am tired of it." The clinician says that it seemed as if the problem wasn't about rubbing Lisa's back, it was about something else; that Lisa looked sad and disappointed, but it did not seem to be about her back. The mother's anger leaves her, and she says tenderly: "I know you are sad, Lisa. It's about his leaving, I know. Come sit on my lap." Lisa sits on the mother's lap, and the mother cuddles her. Lisa kisses her and the mother kisses Lisa back. Lisa sits quietly, clearly comforted by her mother. When the therapist leaves, mother and daughter walk her to the door holding hands.

2. **The clinician points out to the parent, in a serious and interested way and without anger, how the child feels when criticized or called by derogatory names.**

   Example: Gabriel, age 5, and his mother had a difficult day. Gabriel chased his 2-year-old sister with a shopping cart and the little girl ran into the parking lot just as a car was coming by, barely missing her. As she recounts the event, the mother says: "He is just like his father. Do you remember the film *The Evil Seed*? Sometimes I think I gave birth to a child like that." As she speaks, Gabriel approaches his sister and hits her. The mother screams: "Stop hitting your sister! I won't let you murder us!" Gabriel walks away and starts pulling a baby doll apart. The clinician says: "Gabriel, you are showing us how you feel when your mom speaks like that about you." There is a silence. The clinician adds: "I see that it upsets you very much when your mom speaks of you that way." The mother says: "I said he would murder us, didn't I?" The clinician answers: "That is what I heard, and that is what Gabriel also heard. Children really believe what their mothers say." The mother says: "Sometimes I forget he is just a little boy, he reminds me of his father so much." The clinician says: "Gabriel, your mom is telling us that she forgets that you are only a little boy. She is angry at your dad, and then she gets angry at you, but you are just a little boy who needs to learn how not to hurt your sister. I am here to help your mom remember that you are only a little boy and to help you learn what to do with your angry and scary feelings."

3. **The clinician puts into words how the child is responding nonverbally to the parent's criticism, speaking to both parent and child in a supportive and sympathetic manner.**

Example: The clinician has to cut the home visit short because the family has acquired a new cat that triggers a severe allergic reaction. When the clinician explains to Joshua, age 3, that she needs to go home because the cat is making her sick, he starts crying loudly. Between sobs, he says he wants the clinician to stay and play. The mother yells at him: "You are a crybaby! Don't do this to me! She has to go home, and that's all." The clinician comes close to Joshua and says: "Joshua, I know you are very sad that I have to leave and take the toys with me. I know you thought I would stay longer, and I am very sorry that I am sick and have to go." Joshua stops crying. The clinician adds that she will talk to his mother to figure out a place where they can all meet so the cat won't make her sick. She says, "I'll see you next week and bring the toys again, and then we'll play some more." Joshua bends down and quietly helps to put the toys away. The mother tells the clinician: "I see what you did. You acknowledged his feelings, and then you let him feel them." The clinician asks: "Do you think it is OK for him to feel his feelings? I mean, not stop crying right away?" The mother laughs and says: "Of course it is. He has to feel what he is going to feel, and I can't stop it—nor maybe should I. OK, I see what I am doing. This is good, this is good." The clinician says lightly: "You think maybe Joshua would like to hear it directly from you?" The mother says to Joshua: "I am sorry I yelled at you, Joshua. Of course you are sad that (clinician's name) is leaving. But we will make sure that we find another place to play so the cat won't make her sick. Then we can all play together again."

4. **The clinician includes the child in the conversation, speaking to the child's experience, rephrasing the parent's criticism in child-appropriate terms, and/or encouraging the parent and child to talk about what happened between them.**

> *Example:* Linda's mother begins the session by saying that she is furious at the child. She glares at her daughter, and Linda, age 5, looks down at her lap with no expression on her face. The mother tells Linda to tell what happened. Linda is silent. The clinician says to the mother that, because she is so very mad at Linda, it might be better if she were the one who tells what happened. The mother explains that Linda's teacher told her that Linda was playing with a boy in the "pretend house," and wanted a boy to get on top of her. The boy did not want to, and Linda tried to force him until he started to cry and the teacher intervened. The mother now says angrily to Linda: "Look at me while I speak, Linda," but Linda continues to stare at her lap. The clinician says: "Linda, do you know what your mom is talking about?" Linda comes over to her, buries her head in the clinician's chest, and shakes her head yes. The clinician says that her mother gets very upset when she hears that Linda makes boys lie on top of her. Linda says: "I know, but I can't help it. I try to, but I can't."
>
> The mother continues to look angrily at Linda. The clinician says to Linda: "I know you feel you can't help it." She says: "And everyone gets so mad at me." The clinician nods her head, and they all sit in silence for a moment. Then the clinician says that it is hard for grown-ups when they see children do things that are for grown-ups, not for children. Linda nods and remains silent. She then looks down at her lap, and says: "Mom and K. (mother's former boyfriend) were in bed, they were naked, and they were fighting really, really loud, and mommy had a knife and the police came and mommy told me to stay in bed and she went outside."

The mother's eyes open wide, but she says nothing. The clinician comments that it must have been very, very scary. Linda says: "I was scared that he would hurt my mommy. And now we see him every morning before school and it scares me." The mother says: "That's a lie, Linda. We haven't seen him in a long time." Linda looks down at her lap again, her eyes filling with tears. The clinician says softly that she could not imagine Linda would lie about something that upset her so much, and asks the mother what she thought Linda was thinking about. The mother explains that a while back they used to see K. on the street on the way to school, and she would stop and talk to him because he is the father of her younger child and she thought he should see his daughter. Linda interrupts the mother's description to say she was scared K. would hurt the mother. The mother says sharply: "He won't, Linda." The clinician says: "But Linda can't be sure of that. She has seen him hurt you before, and she is very, very worried. Why would she think that he is any different now?" Linda starts to sob loudly.

The mother says that she did not realize it upset Linda so much, that it had not happened in a long time. Speaking both to mother and daughter, the clinician says that it is clearly very much in Linda's mind, and it upsets her very much. Looking at the child, she adds that Linda thinks about it at school because she worries about it so much on the way there, and then at school she plays the things she remembers. Linda's sobbing subsides, and there is a silence. The clinician asks the mother if there is a way she could help Linda not worry so much. The mother says that she easily could. If she sees K. on the street, she would not stop. The clinician asks Linda if that would help, and Linda nods "yes." The clinician says that it is very important for Linda to really be able to count on that. The mother tells Linda she promised that she would never stop, that she did not know it scared Linda so much, and that now she understood. The clinician asks Linda how that sounded. Linda nods her head. The mother asks her if she feels better, and she nods again.

5. **The clinician helps parent and child search for alternative behaviors that will allow the child and/or the parent to express emotion without engaging in hurtful or socially inappropriate behavior.**

Example: In the example just described, Linda says to the clinician, when the mother goes to the bathroom: "But Mommy is still mad at me for playing with that boy."

The clinician answers that she is probably right, and adds that it is good to talk about that. The clinician adds that she is worried because she knows that Linda's play scares other children and scares her too because it gets her in trouble. Linda nods. The clinician suggests that Linda could try to not make boys lie on top of her at school or anywhere else, but she could play that game with the dolls or the toy animals, and she could do that also during their time together. Linda asks: "It's OK with my mommy?" The clinician says they could ask her mommy when she comes back. She asks Linda how she feels about trying to play they way she suggested, and the child says softly that she would try. When the mother comes back, the clinician describes the previous conversation and the plan, and the mother agrees.

Then Linda goes to the bathroom, and while she is gone the mother says that both Linda and her younger daughter cry very hard when she drops them off at school.

This reminds the clinician of a recent conversation with the children's teacher, who complained that the mother drops them off at school abruptly and without saying good-bye. The clinician now tells the mother that the school transition is very hard on kids, that they just learned how much Linda worries on her way to school, and that probably her younger daughter worries too. She suggests that being around for a few minutes, saying good-bye, and telling the children that she would pick them up at the end of the day would be very reassuring for them. It would help them feel less worried about letting the mother out of their sight. The mother says she would think about it and maybe she would try.

6. **The clinician encourages the child to put his or her feelings into words in response to the parent's behavior.**

   Example: Yael, age 4, says: "My mommy told me she will cut my fingers off."

The clinician expresses surprise and interest in knowing what happened. The mother explains that she had been talking to her nephew about how in her home country, in years past, they punished people who stole by cutting their fingers off. She stresses that she had not told Yael anything about cutting her fingers off. The clinician asks Yael about her fear of having her fingers cut off. Yael says: "My mommy will cut my fingers off if I'm bad." She goes to hide under a table as she speaks. The clinician remembers that Yael has been having problems at the day care center for taking things out of the other children's cubbies. She leans under the table and says: "Were you thinking that your mom will cut your fingers off because she gets angry when you take things from the children's cubbies at school?" Yael nods in agreement. The clinician tells the mother that Yael seems so scared that she is hiding under the table. The mother laughs nervously and says that she would never do something like that to Yael. She reaches under the table and asks Yael to come sit on her lap. As she hugs Yael, the mother tells her that she will never tell that old story again because she can see that it frightens Yael. The clinician approves of the idea, and tells the mother that at Yael's age children can't always tell the difference between reality and a story, and they often believe stories are real and could happen to them.

7. **When the parent seems unresponsive to all other intervention strategies, the clinician urges the parent, politely but with conviction, not to speak in those critical terms because it has a negative effect on the child.**

Example: Sandy, age 2, is rather clumsy. She bumps into things, drops the objects that she is holding, and is slow at mastering age-appropriate gross motor skills. Her mother, who is quite athletic, feels embarrassed by her clumsy daughter and has taken to calling her "klutz." The clinician has tried to address this topic, but the mother seems oblivious to it. In one session, Sandy trips over a toy and falls down, hitting her head on the coffee table. She cries briefly but gets up and keeps moving. The mother says: "That happened to you because you are a klutz." The clinician says: "I know you'd like her to be more agile, but children develop at different rates. I strongly recommend that you not call her a klutz any more. She takes what you say very seriously, and your giving her a label will only make her self-conscious. She'll think this is the way she'll stay forever." The mother says: "Well, isn't it? Do you think she can possibly grow out of it?" The clinician says: "I certainly think she can grow out of it, but even if she doesn't, she can either feel terrible for who she is or she can take it in stride and take pleasure in all the other things she knows how to do." The mother says nothing, but looks thoughtful.

Domain IX: Relationship With the Perpetrator/Absent Parent

Children who have witnessed domestic violence between their parents and who then experience the father's departure from the home are subjected to the dual stresses of exposure to violence between their attachment figures and subsequent separation or loss of one of them, most frequently the father. From the perspective of attachment theory, witnessing the mother being attacked and injured involves a profound assault on the child's capacity to trust her as a reliable protector. When the child most needs her proximity, contact, and reassurance, the mother cannot be available because she herself is in physical and emotional need and perhaps danger. When the attacker is also an attachment figure (as in the case of a father or stepfather, or when the mother is also violent), the child's mental representations of the parent are split between love and terror. Young children exposed to domestic violence cannot form or sustain internal representations of violent parents as a secure base that provides safety and protection. On the contrary, it is the parents who engender fear while simultaneously eliciting a strong wish to rely on their protection. For infants in the first year of life, who are in the process of forming and consolidating attachments, one parent's departure from the home presents the additional challenge of maintaining the memory of that parent across gaps of days or even weeks between visits. They need to reconnect emotionally and cognitively with that parent at sporadic intervals, which in turn tax the child's emotional and cognitive resources.

The need to retain an image of their parents as loving and protective forces children into costly coping strategies that must be changed as the situations they face change. For example, if they are spending time with their father, they may suppress memories of his violence and adopt a view of the mother as the guilty party. When they spend time with the mother, the reverse may hold true. As a result, the child who has witnessed domestic violence experiences different emotions that serve a defensive function in relation to one another. These include longing for the absent father, fear of him, and imitation of him through identification with the aggressor. With regard to the mother, the child may experience fear, anger, and blame, which coexist with fear of losing her and protectiveness of her. These conflicting feelings are exacerbated by the actual behavior of the mother and the father when they vie with each other for the child's love, loyalty, and approval by blaming their partner and asking the young child to join them in their perception of the family drama.

The goal of the intervention is to facilitate the formation of realistic ambivalence as a psychological achievement in the child's relationship toward the abusive parent. In other words, the clinician strives to enable the child to form a more balanced and integrated internal representation of the abusive parent, involving a conscious acknowledgement that the violent parent engenders love, fear, and anger simultaneously. This goal is applicable to the child's relationship with violent mothers as well as fathers because a significant subset of battered women report that they are themselves violent toward the partner, and physically punitive toward the child.

This section focuses on the child's conflicting feelings toward the absent violent parent, most commonly the father, because of the importance of facilitating an ongoing father–child relationship whenever this goal does not interfere with the child's and the mother's safety. This goal necessarily requires working with the mother's feelings toward her estranged partner and the way she expresses these feelings to the child. Mothers going through difficult divorces often need help in remembering that the child's relationship with the father is separate from the marital relationship and should be respected in its own right. Mothers who are traumatized, anxious, or depressed by domestic violence may be even more likely to blur the differences between the spousal and the parental relationships.

At the same time, the reality of the mother's experience of violence needs to be acknowledged and legitimized. Many battered women are reluctant to allow their children to spend time with their violent fathers for fear that the father will endanger the child or paint a distorted and negative picture of the mother that will make the child angry and suspicious toward her. These fears are well founded in the context of the violence the mothers suffered from their partners, and they should be neither minimized nor attributed to manipulative efforts by the mother to alienate the child from the father. Maternal reports about worrisome paternal behavior toward the child should be given serious consideration and referred to the appropriate legal channels for further evaluation and action. The clinician should keep in mind that domestic violence often co-occurs with child abuse, and that abusive partners can well be abusive fathers and/or engage in domestic violence with their new partners in front of the child. The child's and mother's physical safety takes precedence over all other considerations, and the clinician must take prompt action to help the mother protect herself and the child when there is evidence of ongoing violence or inappropriate behavior by the child's father.

Some battered women continue to have loving feelings toward their abusive partners and harbor hopes that he will change and that the family can be reunified. These wishes can alternate abruptly with rage and fear as memories of the assaults become salient. This alternation of feelings reflects the mother's lingering traumatization. It is of utmost importance that the clinician does not take a position in favor or against reconciliation. The clinician's role is not to tell the mother what life decisions she should make, but rather to explore with her the different facets of her feelings as she describes them to the clinician, and to consistently bring the mother's attention to the implications of her experiences for her child, always supporting decisions that are consistent with safety.

When the father or perpetrator becomes involved in assessment or treatment, this therapeutic attitude must also be maintained. In order to do this work, the challenge for the clinician is to, at one and the same time, remember clearly the details of the violence and the hurt that were inflicted, without losing sight of the more positive attributes that the violent partner might also have. To enable the child and the mother to develop a realistic ambivalence about the father, the clinicians must first achieve it themselves.

ITEMS AND CLINICAL EXAMPLES

1. **When the child refers to frightening scenes of violence and anger, the clinician encourages the child to speak about what happened and elicits the feelings experienced by the child, encouraging a dialogue between mother and child.**

   Example: Prior to the session, the clinician received a message from Dahlia's mother that her estranged husband had hit her the day before because she refused to resume their relationship. The mother wanted to inform the clinician so it would not take her by surprise during the session. At the beginning of the session, the clinician tells Dahlia, age 5, that her mom said something scary had happened. Dahlia nods in agreement. The clinician asks what happened. Dahlia says: "My dad came to the house and said he wanted my mom to cook him something. She was tired and in bed. I wanted to go up to her bedroom but he told me to stay in the kitchen and went upstairs. When I went to Mom's room, her piggy bank was broken and all over the floor. My dad slapped my mom." The clinician asks what happened then. The child says: "I was crying and telling my mom not to call the police." The clinician asks about this, and Dahlia answers: "I don't want my daddy to go to jail." The clinician asks what happened next. Dahlia says: "My daddy told my mom to get out and started throwing her clothes down the stairs. I was scared my mommy was going to leave." The clinician asks the mother what she thinks about what Dahlia is saying, and the mother replies: "I will never leave you, Dahlia. I made your dad leave because he hurts me, but if I go anywhere, I will always take you with me." Dahlia nods, and the clinician asks her to tell her more. Dahlia says: "I went to the bathroom to get a towel so my mom could dry her eyes. She was crying so hard." The clinician asks: "You were trying to help your mom feel better. What about you? Were you crying?" Dahlia says: "When I went to the bathroom to get a towel for my mom, I wiped my eyes also. My brain was going like this" (the child moved her finger around her forehead). The clinician asks what that was like and the child says she does not know. The clinician asks: "Were you having a lot of thoughts?" Dahlia yes, but adds that she cannot remember any of the thoughts. "I don't remember how it was." After some more talk, the clinician suggests that the mother tell Dahlia what will happen next. The mother tells Dahlia that her dad is not in jail, but he will stay away from the house and not come there to pick her up anymore, and they will find a way for Dahlia to continue seeing her daddy. Dahlia looks sad. The clinician says that her mom had tried a lot of things, but they haven't worked and her mom does not want to be scared any more. Dahlia says: "I don't want my mom to be scared, and she was scared yesterday." The adults agree. Dahlia adds: "My daddy is causing trouble. I love him, but he drinks too much and he causes a lot of trouble."

2. **When the child speaks about the absent father in a way that indicates a misunderstanding of the situation, the clinician invites the mother to elicit the child's thinking and to correct faulty perceptions, or does so when the mother is unable to.**

> *Example:* When she arrives for the home visit, the clinician finds Sylvia, age 4, playing ball in the backyard. They start throwing the ball back and forth for a few minutes. Suddenly the child says: "My daddy's dead." The clinician replies that she did not think her daddy was dead, but she could understand why Sylvia thought so because he had not called her for a long time. As they get to the apartment, Sylvia asks her mother for paper and pencil and announces: "I am going to write a letter for my daddy." As she makes random letters across the page, she says aloud: "Daddy, where are you? Why aren't you picking me up?" She stops abruptly, puts her skates on, and skates out of the room. While the child is out of the room, the clinician tells the mother about Sylvia's idea that her father is dead, and the mother expresses sadness that he has not seen the child in a long time. When Sylvia skates back into the room, the clinician says: "I think you went looking for your daddy. Your mommy just told me that he is not dead, but he is not coming to see you anymore, and it is very sad." Sylvia says: "I am now going to dictate a letter. You write: 'Daddy, where are you? You used to call me your princess. Daddy, why did you go to the moon?'"

3. **When the child says or does things that express divided loyalties between the parents, the clinician speaks for the different feelings of the child, enlisting the mother's help, when possible, in giving the child permission to love both parents.**

> *Example:* Carina's mother seems unusually strained and upset with her child as the session begins. The clinician comments on it, and the mother replies that it had been a very tiring week and that earlier in the day, when she picked up Carina from school, the child had thrown sand at her. The clinician asks Carina, age 4, what was happening to make her throw sand at her mother.

Carina smiles coyly, and the mother says Carina had several tantrums that week and it all began with the Sunday visit to her father. She adds that Carina had a very hard time saying good-bye to her dad. The clinician says to Carina: "You really miss your dad." Carina nods. The clinician continues: "You really love him and it's hard to say good-bye to him." The mother interjects that Carina was not able to go to the jungle gym with her dad because they ran out of time, and adds that when he brought her back he yelled at the mother for 10 minutes for presumably keeping Carina away from him, even though he misses half of his visits and Carina is disappointed when she does not see him. Carina says: "I love my daddy best and I want to spend more time with him." The mother looks visibly pained. The clinician says: "Right now you love your daddy best, and you are angry at your mom because you think that she is keeping you away from him." Carina looks intently at the clinician. The clinician says: "Maybe your mom can talk to you about it." The mother says: "I know you love your dad and you miss him and it would be great if you could see him as much as you want, but he lives far away and he does not come to all his visits. That is not my fault." Carina says: "I went to the park with my dad." The clinician says it was good that she and her dad could do something she wanted, and that it was hard when her mom and dad did not agree about the visits when she wanted so much to be with her dad and it was so hard to say good-bye to him. Carina says: "Someday I am going to go on a plane and visit my dad and Dad said I could call him anytime." Under her breath, the mother comments that it is up to the court to decide if Carina can go on a plane to visit him, and that he makes promises that he does not keep. To Carina, she says that someday she would get to travel on a plane, but that it would be with her mom and that right now Carina is too little to go on a plane by herself and her dad was not ready to come and get her on a plane. The clinician says: "Your mom and dad are thinking hard about what they want for you, because both of them love you a lot but they don't agree, and your mom wants to make sure that when they tell you that something will happen, it will really happen, so you won't be disappointed." The child looks very attentive. The conversation continues in this vein for some time. As they leave, mother and child are visibly relaxed and affectionate with each other.

4. **When the child expresses anger at the father, the clinician empathizes with the child's feelings but leaves open the possibility of change for the better.**

   Example: Jamal, age 4, says that he wants to cut his father up and bake him in the oven. The clinician says: "How come?" Jamal says: "He threw a cup at my mother, and it hit her knee." The clinician says: "That's a very scary thing to do. No wonder you are angry at him." Jamal says: "My dad doesn't know the rules." The clinician says: "No, he doesn't. It takes some people a long time to know the rules. Maybe one day your dad can learn if he really tries."

5. **When the child engages in inappropriate behavior learned from the father, the clinician makes the connection between the father's and the child's behavior, explains that even fathers can make mistakes, and tries to enlist the mother's cooperation in this effort.**

   Example: Sammy, age 3, says to his mother: "I will kill you. I will shoot you."

   The mother does not answer. Sammy adds: "You whore." The mother's face reddens.

   The clinician says: "Sammy, your mom told me that your daddy talked to her that way. I know you love your daddy, but you can't talk that way. Your dad makes a mistake when he does that, and we don't want you to make the same mistake. Your mommy is not a whore and nobody should kill or shoot her." The mother looks relieved. The clinician tells the mother that she will help Sammy by standing up firmly for herself when he says things like that because he does not know any better and needs to learn from her what is right and what is wrong.

   Example: Andy, age 4, kicks his mother soon after hearing her tell the clinician that she left Andy's father because he kicked her.

The clinician says: "Andy, you are remembering how your daddy kicked your mom and then she decided the two of you could not live with him anymore." Andy puts his hands over his ears. The clinician keeps quiet, and when Andy uncovers his ears, she says quietly: "It hurts to remember that." Andy looks at her sadly. The clinician says: "Your mommy will not leave you even if you kick her. You are her little boy and she will never leave you. But your dad kicked her because he forgot how to use his words. I come to see you so that you remember how to use your words even when you are angry."

6. **When the child's behavior suggests guilt about the father's leaving, the clinician encourages the mother to explain that this is not the child's fault, or takes the initiative in doing so.**

   Example: The mother of Saul, age 5, expresses regret that her behavior drove her husband away. She states that she got used to the hitting but could not stand it when he had an affair. She says that she should have known better and should not have confronted and talked back to her husband, and adds that her older daughter knew about the affair but did not tell her in order to protect her. The clinician comments that children often feel responsible for their father's leaving. The mother's face lights up and she says: "That's it! Saul and her sister are always saying that if they had not been so bad their father would not have left." The clinician suggests that this might be a good thing to talk about as a family, how each of them thinks that if they did things differently, the father would not have left.

7. **When the child expresses longing or sadness about the absent father, the clinician empathizes with these feelings and encourages the mother to do the same.**

   Example: The mother of Lidia, age 4, reports that her father will be living with his grandmother in another town and came over to say good-bye, but was absent-minded and preoccupied during his brief visit and left abruptly. For hours afterward, Lidia kept asking "Where is my daddy?" The clinician now asks if Lidia knows that her dad left, and the mother says she doesn't know. Lidia looks up

from her play and says, very upset: "My dad is gone?!" The
mother looks helplessly at the clinician, and asks if she can tell
Lidia what happened, adding: "I know I should, but I don't know
how. Help me tell her." The clinician asks what she would like
Lidia to know, and the mother, after hesitating briefly, says to
Lidia: "Your dad is very sad and needs to go stay with his grandmother because it helps him feel better." Lidia asks: "Is he coming back today?" The mother answers that his grandmother's
house is far away and he will be gone for a long time. Lidia's affect
becomes very subdued and her eyes fill with tears. The mother
looks at the clinician as if asking for help. The clinician says: "I
know you are very sad that your dad had to leave and he did not
spend much time with you during his visit." Lidia says: "He
didn't even say good-bye." The clinician says she knows that made
her sad. She nods sadly. There is a silence. The clinician says:
"You know, Lidia, you are right that people should say good-bye.
Saying good-bye is very important. But many grown-ups don't
know that. They don't know that saying good-bye is very important. I think your dad doesn't know how to say good-bye because
it is a hard thing to do. I know that hurt you very much, but your
dad loves you even though he did not say good-bye."

8. When the child expresses identification with the aggressive aspects of the father, the clinician speaks to the child's underlying confusion and fear.

Example: Paulo's mother is speaking about being at the end of her
rope and feeling unable to cope with Paulo, who has just been
expelled from child care because he hit a child. Paulo, age 4, hits
his mother and quickly bites the clinician on the arm when she
tries to intervene. The clinician says: "You can't do that, Paulo.
You can't hit your mom and you can't bite me." Paulo replies: "I
want to grow up to be bad like my daddy." The clinician says:
"You are missing your dad but you are also scared of him. He hurt
you and your mommy." Paulo moves away and starts playing by
himself. Later in the session, the clinician says: "Your mom had
to leave your dad because he hurt her, but she doesn't want to
leave you. She loves you and wants to help you, and that is why I
come here." Paulo says: "Is Daddy bad? I want to be a good boy."

The clinician says: "Your daddy hurt you and your mommy. Your mommy is teaching you not to hurt anybody, and I am here to help her."

9. **When the mother criticizes the father or brings up his faults in front of the child, the clinician finds a way of reframing the negative picture of the father, so that the seriousness of the situation is acknowledged, but the child's loving feelings for the father are supported and legitimized.**

Example: The mother of Mandy, age 4, has filed a Child Protective Services (CPS) report stating that Mandy's father sexually abused the child. She also has a restraining order against the father. CPS doubts the veracity of the report. In the session, the mother bursts into tears and reports: "I told the child welfare worker how enraged Mandy's father became when I asked him to be more careful when Mandy climbed out of the sunroof of his car. And you know what the worker said? He said that it is a two-way street. Mandy's father has molested my little boy and has physically attacked me. It is not a two-way street!" The clinician speaks supportively to the mother, who calms down. Mandy is playing with a toy cannon, pretends that he has been shot by one of the cannons, and covers his face with a cloth as he is sprawled on the floor. The clinician tells the mother that Mandy looks "seriously hurt," and suggests that they drag him over to the pillows to see how badly he was injured. The mother joins in the play and says: "Mandy looks seriously injured indeed!" Mother and clinician check the child's limbs and find the "injury." The clinician says that some good medicine and some magic words will help Mandy get better, and she and the mother minister to Mandy. They agree that the magic word is "Abracadabra," and pronounce it over Mandy, who then takes the kerchief off his face with a big smile and announces: "I am all better." Later in the session, the clinician says to Mandy: "Your mommy is afraid that your daddy is hurting you, and she is trying very hard to make sure you are safe." Mandy says: "My daddy scares me sometimes, but he's nice." The clinician says: "It's confusing when your daddy scares you but he's also nice."

Domain X: Ghosts in the Nursery: The Intergenerational Transmission of Psychopathology

The image of ghosts in the nursery was coined by Selma Fraiberg nearly 30 years ago to describe the parents' enactment with their child of their repressed experiences of helplessness and fear (Fraiberg, Adelson, & Shapiro, 1975). The ghosts represent the unconscious repetition of the past in the present through punitive or neglectful caregiving practices, which the now-parent internalized as a child in an effort at self-protection by becoming like the abusive parent. Parents who are haunted by the ghosts of their early experiences routinely fail to recognize, empathize with, and respond to their child's signals of need for care and protection. Instead, they perceive the child through the lens of negative attributions that mimic the perceived characteristics of the punitive or neglectful caregivers from their past. In essence, the child becomes a transference object, losing his or her own developmental and individual features while standing for a figure from the past. Children subjected to this kind of parental distortion progressively internalize a sense of self as unworthy and undeserving of love that can derail the course of healthy development (Bowlby, 1980; Lieberman, 1997, 1999; Silverman & Lieberman, 1999). This process involves the transmission from parent to child of the defense mechanism described by Anna Freud (1936/1966) as identification with the aggressor. This communication from parent to child comprises the psychologically damaging pole of the intergenerational transmission of psychological patterns that, in more benevolent family circumstances, can be represented as the influence on development of angels in the nursery.

In their pioneering work with mental health disorders in infancy, Fraiberg and her colleagues attributed the havoc caused by the ghosts of the parental past not to the actual events but to the repression of the *affects* associated with frightening early memories. These parental affects are often freely expressed toward the child in the context of child–parent psychotherapy. The parent may behave during the sessions as if he or she were transformed back into a young child, helpless and terrified but endeavoring to master these feelings through harsh criticism, emotional withdrawal, and other behaviors that signal an identification with the abusive parental figures from their past.

The initial assessment sessions are geared at gaining an understanding of the childhood roots of the parent's current difficulties in caregiving. The clinician can use this information to develop tentative hypotheses linking the parent's early experiences of stress or trauma with current maladaptive caregiving practices. When the parent has been the victim of domestic violence, the emotional impact of this assault or series of assaults compounds the enduring effect of early adversities. The child who witnesses the violence often becomes associated with it in the parent's mind. Victimized mothers often engage in an unconscious equation of their children with their perpetrators, attributing to the child the characteristics of danger and brutality that properly belong to their partners (Silverman & Lieberman, 1999).

The preliminary hypotheses developed during the assessment period are not necessarily shared with the parent, but they can be kept in mind for confirmation or disconfirmation from the material that emerges during treatment. When the interventions described in earlier sections of the manual are not effective in promoting parental attitudes and behaviors that are more developmentally appropriate, the clinician should consider switching to an exploration of how the parent's past is influencing current perceptions and behaviors toward the child. Time-limited individual collateral sessions are the format of choice in these circumstances. If a few individual sessions indicate that the parent needs more in-depth psychotherapy, the clinician may choose to expand the scope of the treatment to include ongoing individual sessions with the parent in addition to child–parent psychotherapy, or may refer the parent to another practitioner.

The capacity to integrate the good and bad parts of a loved person into a sturdy sense of object constancy has long been considered the hallmark of the adult capacity to love (Fairbairn, 1954; Freud, 1923/1966; Kernberg, 1976; Klein, 1932; Mahler, Pine, & Bergman, 1975; Winnicott, 1962). Helping the parent become more conscious of the pain associated with early experiences should not be an end in itself. Whenever possible, the clinician should endeavor to help the parent remember and hold in mind the multifaceted nature of his or her early relationships. Compassion and forgiveness for the imperfect parents of the past cannot be decreed by clinical caveat, but the parent–child relationship in the present will be immeasurably helped by the current parent's ability to reconnect with the angels while making peace with the ghosts in his or her nursery.

Timing is a crucial element in increasing the likelihood that an intervention will be effective in promoting inner growth and behavioral change. This is particularly the case when the clinician addresses aspects of the parent's life that are laden with pain, anger, shame, or helplessness, and when the parent has been engaged in protracted efforts at fending off these negative feelings through the use of displacement, projection, and denial. For this reason, it is difficult to itemize specific clinical strategies for linking early conflicts with current parenting problems. The following section provides a beginning approach through clinical examples, but case-centered supervision is needed to acquire or enhance clinical skill in this area.

ITEMS AND CLINICAL EXAMPLES

1. **The clinician inquires explicitly about caregiving adults or specific experiences that made the parent feel frightened or in danger while growing up.**

    Example: Lenny, age 2, has been expelled from day care because he bit another child for the fourth time and the parents have complained that he is a danger for their children. During the assessment, Lenny's mother, Mrs. O'Brian, describes extensive domestic violence perpetrated by Lenny's father, who is now out of the home and has an unpredictable pattern of visits with Lenny on approximately a monthly basis. Mrs. O'Brian is worried about these visits because she believes that her husband is using them to turn Lenny against her. She says that Lenny has prolonged tantrums when he returns from visits with his father, refuses to be comforted by her, and hits her and kicks her when she tries to hold him. After eliciting a detailed account of present circumstances, the clinician asks: "What were things like for you when you were growing up?" Mrs. O'Brian says that her parents divorced when she was a baby and she never knew her father. She adds: "I have been thinking of going back with my husband because I don't want Lenny to grow up without a father, like I did." The clinician replies: "Given what you told me about how frightened you are of him, you must feel very strongly that you want Lenny to have a father to consider getting back with him." The mother agrees. The clinician asks: "What do you remember about growing up without a father?" The mother answers: "I felt humiliated when the other children talked about their fathers and

I had nothing to say." The clinician asks: "Humiliated? How come? Did you think it was your fault that he left?" The mother answers: "Maybe not my fault, but I thought that if he loved me he would have stayed." The clinician asks: "Do you have any ideas about why he did not love you?" The mother says sadly: "I was not good enough." She has tears in her eyes. The clinician makes the link with Lenny by asking: "Do you want to make sure Lenny does not feel like he is not good enough to have his father stay, like you did?" The mother nods in silent agreement.

This exchange illustrates the clinician's efforts to uncover the aspects of the mother's early experience that are associated with her child's current difficulties. The preliminary hypotheses, which are based on the mother's report of her self-blame for her father's abandonment, involved the following set of related premises: the mother's romantic involvement with a man who abused her was based on her conviction that she deserved no better because she was not good enough to keep her father's love; she deserved to be punished for not being good enough; she wanted to protect her child from the self-blame and suffering of growing up without a father. Reuniting with Lenny's father would confirm and perpetuate her self-concept as undeserving of love while ostensibly protecting her child from the same fate. The clinician believed that Lenny was adopting the mother's distorted perception of herself by blaming her for his father's absence and punishing her by hitting and kicking her in much the same ways he had witnessed his father doing to her. Mrs. O'Brian's failure to set limits to Lenny's aggression simultaneously confirmed the child's perception that she was "bad" and left him unable to regulate his intense traumatic stress responses from witnessing the violence, grief at his father's absence, and anger at his mother as the perceived culprit for what befell him. Having a "bad" mother is, in children's minds, inevitably linked to being "bad" oneself because one deserves no better. These hypotheses informed the clinician's pursuit of intervention strategies designed to help the mother realize that her father left her not because she was unlovable but because he could not love; that witnessing violence frightened

Lenny and made him feel that he could not trust his parents to love and protect him; and that in stopping Lenny firmly but calmly from expressing anger through aggression, she was helping him to feel loved and protected by showing him that she would not leave him alone with his unmanageable feelings. In intervening calmly but firmly to contain Lenny's aggression his mother was also able to disconfirm, in Lenny's mind and her own, the belief that she was not lovable and that she deserved punishment.

2. **When the parent engages with the child in an exchange that evokes early experiences of feeling unloved, frightened, or unprotected, the clinician links the present situation to those memories in an effort to make the parent aware of the early roots of the present situation.**

> *Example:* In a joint child–parent session 2 months into the treatment, Mrs. O'Brian (see previous example) is telling the clinician that Lenny's father did not show up for a visit with the child. She says: "All he cares about is himself. He doesn't give a damn about Lenny. I prepared Lenny for the visit, had him all dressed up, and we were waiting and waiting. He did not even call. He simply did not show up." Lenny is playing with some blocks making a tower. Listening to his mother, he kicks the tower and makes the tower fall down. The clinician says to Lenny: "Your mommy is telling me that your daddy did not come to see you. She is upset because she knows you wanted to see him." Lenny goes to the window and tries to reach it by stepping on the armchair that is next to it. The mother retrieves him, saying: "Don't do that! You are going to fall!" Lenny shrieks, flails at her to get down, and hits her after she puts him on the floor. The mother sits back down on her chair without reacting. The clinician says to Lenny: "No hitting Mommy. Mommy was trying to help you. She knows that you want your daddy." Lenny goes back to the blocks and continues playing. The clinician says to the mother: "I can't help but think of what you told me about growing up without your father and how sad that made you." The mother nods silently. The therapist continues: "When you were waiting for his father to come, do you think you were having the old feelings of waiting for your father all over again?"

The clinician used the mother's intense reaction to Lenny's father's missed visit as a port of entry to link her feelings in the present to her early unfulfilled longing for her father. The mother's unconscious equation of Lenny's father with her own father prevented her from remaining emotionally available to Lenny while they were waiting for his father and during the days that followed. Her feelings of abandonment, self-blame, and anger interfered with her ability to protect the child from the failed expectation of seeing his father. By introducing a bridge between the present and the past, the clinician was suggesting that the mother's response could be understood in a broader context than the concrete circumstances of the missed visit.

The chains of associations linking the present with the past need not be fully elucidated for therapeutic gains to take place. By its very nature, child–parent psychotherapy involves a constant balance between attention to the child–parent relationship and the child's and the parent's individual experience. Emotional growth accrues from the accumulation of different interventions within a context of consistent emotional support. When skillfully timed, interventions linking the present with the past can be transformative even when brief because parents continue to reflect on them after the session and use them to increase their understanding of themselves and of the child.

Domain XI: Angels in the Nursery: Benevolent Influences in the Parent's Past

Parents are able to support their children's development even amidst adverse conditions when their sense of self-worth informs their commitment to the child's well-being. This sense of personal worth is rooted in early exchanges with important adults that were suffused with a sense of heightened intimacy because the child felt thoroughly understood, accepted, and protected. The often silent presence of benevolent influences in the parent's past has been likened to "angels in the nursery" (W. Harris, personal communication, April 23, 2003) because loving experiences are transmitted from one generation to the next in the form of caregiving practices that affirm the child's sense of being cherished and instill trust in the value of human relationships.

Traumatic experiences often block parental access to early experiences that nourished their self-esteem by making them feel loved and deserving of care and protection. Although the ultimate goal of child–parent psychotherapy is to enhance the child's mental health, a simultaneous focus on the parent's subjective experience is necessary to enlist parental motivation and therapeutic collaboration on behalf of the child. Enabling the parent to remember experiences of nurturing and protection in their early life is a powerful therapeutic tool because it enriches the parent's sense of self, instills optimism, and promotes hope in the future by holding up a supportive model of the past.

The initial assessment sessions offer a prime opportunity to search for benevolent experiences in the parent's past because the assessment is explicitly devoted to learning about salient aspects of the parent's and the child's life. By asking about caregivers or interpersonal exchanges that made the parent feel loved, the clinician conveys the message that experiences of safety, trust, intimacy, and joy are fundamentally important and worthy of sustained attention. The parent's positive early experiences can then be used as building blocks to support parallel experiences with the child.

Loving early experiences may not be remembered during the assessment sessions when the parent is overwhelmed by the experience of trauma. The clinician may then remain alert for the emergence of this information in the course of the sessions. When the parent remembers moments of intimacy and joy with a caregiver, the clinician may join with the parent's affective experience by highlighting its value in the parent's life. The parent's experience may then be harnessed to the child's emotional needs by drawing parallels that increase parental empathy for the child.

ITEMS AND CLINICAL EXAMPLES

1. **The clinician inquires explicitly about caregiving adults or specific experiences that made the parent feel loved and cared for while growing up.**

   Example: During the initial assessment interview, Mrs. Gowan speaks with intense anger about her husband and her child, 3-year-old Simon, both of whom she describes as "bullies" who are aggressive and impossible to control. In the course of learning about the family's circumstances, the clinician asks the mother about her childhood. Mrs. Gowan describes an abusive mother and an aloof, withdrawn father. The clinician asks: "Was there anybody that you could rely on as a little girl?" The mother remains silent for a long time. Then her face softens and she says:

"I had an aunt who was single and lived with us for a few years. She taught me to read. I used to love sitting next to her on the sofa, holding a book between us. Sometimes she put her arm around me while reading out loud to me. I loved it. She smelled so good." In telling the story, Mrs. Gowan's anger dissipates and she has tears in her eyes. The clinician says gently: "What a beautiful memory to hold on to with all the pain that you are going through." The mother replies: "I had forgotten it until now. My aunt married and left our house when I was 9. I remember crying when she left. She left me a box of the books that we used to read together. I still have them." The clinician asks: "Do you ever read them to Simon?" The mother says: "No. He wouldn't appreciate them." The clinician replies: "Really? Maybe we can help him appreciate them during our work together."

This scene offers a glimmer of hope in the mother's troubled emotional landscape and her angry relationship with her child. By identifying a nurturing figure in Mrs. Gowan's bleak childhood, the clinician facilitated a temporary transformation in the mother's affect, reconnecting her with an early experience of loving intimacy. The clinician also opened the possibility that the mother's pleasurable memories associated with reading with her aunt could be extended to reading with her son, and upheld the hope that this could be a benefit of treatment in the face of the mother's skepticism that her son could appreciate the books that were so meaningful to her while she was growing up.

2. **When the parent remembers an early experience of being loved and cared for, the clinician links this memory with the possibility of making the feeling happen again through exchanges with the child.**

Example: Mr. Gomez, the father of Ronnie, age 4, recalls a scene from his adolescence where his father put a hand on his shoulder and said: "It's OK" after he made a mistake playing football that made his team lose the game. Clearly moved, the father says: "It made me feel that he loved me in spite of my mistake." The clinician asks: "That is such an important feeling. Did he usually behave like that?" Mr. Gomez answers: "Not really. He had a terrible temper and yelled at me a lot. But every once in a while he could make me feel really good. Once he told a kid who was threatening me that he would send him packing if he did that again. I felt so safe. He made me feel important—like he was really busy but he noticed what was happening and took the time to defend me. The kid never bothered me again." After a silence, the clinician asks: "Is that something you want Ronnie to feel with you?"

In this intervention, the clinician helped Mr. Gomez connect the visceral feeling of being accepted and protected by his father with the possibility of offering a similar experience to his son. Mr. Gomez often screamed in anger when Ronnie did something wrong, and felt deeply ashamed of his son's visible fear when this happened. Mr. Gomez associated the memory of his father's acceptance of his mistake playing football with the feeling of being cared for and protected. By introducing Ronnie into this scene, the clinician worked toward an updating of Mr. Gomez's experience of himself from (sometimes) protected son to protective father, and helped to establish a counterweight to the prevailing memories of disapproval and anger.

Domain XII: Saying Good-Bye: Ending the Session, Terminating Treatment

Separating from a person one loves ranks among the most difficult of human experiences. Losing a loved person is the most painful one. Both experiences, each in their distinct fashion, challenge the emotional foundations of the sense of self, and evoke powerful feelings of sadness, anxiety, grief, and anger. When separation and loss occur early in life, or when the person is left without the support of other affectional bonds, the normal course of development can be seriously derailed and adult mental health may be severely compromised (Bowlby, 1973, 1980).

For young children and parents exposed to domestic violence, experiences of separation and loss occur in a traumatizing context because fear for the integrity of the self and of the loved ones is already heightened. Children in the first 5 years of life who witnessed violence against their mothers manifest more symptoms of traumatic stress disorder than children exposed to other forms of trauma (Scheeringa & Zeanah, 1995). Battered women are worried for their children's safety as well as for their own (Peled, 2000). In this context, the abusive parent's or partner's often abrupt and conflict-ridden departure from the home triggers a mixture of relief and guilt about the relief, feelings that compound and complicate the more normative responses of anger and grief.

Young children are particularly vulnerable to the pathogenic potential of traumatic separation or loss because their world view is shaped by the age-appropriate egocentric conviction that their thoughts and actions can make things happen (Piaget, 1959). As a result, they are likely to blame themselves when marital separation occurs. This self-blame occurs with the backdrop of fear of separation and fear of losing the parent's love as the normative anxieties in the first 5 years of life (Fraiberg, 1959). These anxieties become indelibly internalized by the child when real-life events seem to confirm those fears.

These processes set the stage for the child's response to separation from the clinician at the end of each session, and to loss of the clinician when treatment ends. The clinician acquires the role of surrogate attachment figure in the course of the treatment through the consistent focus on providing a haven of safety. The clinician also becomes a transference object that evokes the child's often suppressed feelings and unconscious fantasies about separation and loss.

For these reasons, the good-byes at the end of the session and at the end of treatment, difficult as they are, also represent valuable opportunities for providing the child with corrective emotional experiences of separation and loss. The primary lessons that need to be conveyed are: (a) that separations can be followed by reunions, and (b) that separation and loss do not always mean a loss of love. Through the clinician's responses, the child learns that the image of the loved person can be kept safe inside oneself even when that person is no longer present, and that this image and the memories associated with it can be brought back to mind at times of emotional need and used for comfort and support.

It is important not to downplay the importance of separations, and to announce that "time is up" with enough anticipation that the clinician will not be rushed into a hasty good-bye. The child needs to be given time to prepare inwardly for this important transition and needs unhurried adult support in doing so.

Transitional objects, games that evoke separation and reunion such as "peek-a-boo" and "hide-and-seek," and the parent's support are good strategies in helping preverbal children weather the sadness of a good-bye. For older children, speaking about how they can think of each other and evoking what will happen until they see each other again build continuity of emotional experience between the sessions. Just as good-night rituals help children allay their anxieties before going to sleep, good-bye rituals are very helpful in reassuring the child that the clinician is not leaving out of anger or loss of love for the child.

Similar considerations apply to the end of treatment. From the point of view of the child (and, often, also of the parent), the end of treatment is an arbitrary event that does not take into account the good feelings among the participants. Verbal children invariably ask "Why?" when the clinician announces that she will stop coming in a few weeks. There is no easy answer. It is often helpful to answer the child with a story that gives a brief recapitulation of how things were at the beginning of treatment and how things are now. Such a narrative can emphasize the progress that the child and the parents have made in grappling with difficult feelings. One frequent but unintended byproduct of this approach is that the child (and/or the parent) becomes symptomatic again in an unconscious effort to show the therapist that not all is well and that treatment is still needed. However, if the termination of treatment is addressed with enough time and care, this is usually a short-lived reaction that abates when the feelings of sadness and worry about saying good-bye are given the attention they deserve. Preschoolers are helped by concrete reminders of how much time is left before the final session. This can be done by marking each passing week on a special calendar and counting how many weeks are left.

It is helpful to do something out of the ordinary to mark the last session, and the clinician can work collaboratively with the parent and child to decide whether the last session should be a genuine celebration or whether a more reflective activity would better capture the complex feelings involved in ending an important relationship. Many children decide that they would like to have a party on the last day, and the clinician provides simple refreshments. For other children and parents, the leave-taking may not feel so festive. In these cases, as well as in the cases that are terminated with celebration, it is often helpful to have a Polaroid camera handy so that children can leave with photographs as a concrete reminder of the experience that they and their mothers have shared with the therapist.

ITEMS AND CLINICAL EXAMPLES

1. **The clinician helps the child cope with the separation at the end of the session by announcing that she or he will be leaving soon and by giving the child choices about how to say good-bye. Rituals surrounding separation are very effective in helping children cope with the anxiety of saying good-bye because they create a sense of predictability and control.**

   Example: Reesa, age 3, is playing happily with the clinician and the mother. The clinician says: "You know what? I have to say good-bye in a few more minutes." The child's face becomes somber. The clinician says: "So, when I say good-bye, do you want to open the door or should I?" Reesa says: "I will." The clinician says: "Then what will happen after that? Will we wave good-bye at the door or..." Reesa interrupts, saying: "Go to the bottom of the stairs and look up and say good-bye." The clinician says: "OK, and then what?" Reesa answers: "Then you come back next time," and smiles. As the clinician walks down the stairs, Reesa says: "Wait, I have to go pee!" She turns to the mother, says "I have to go pee!" and races inside, yelling: "Wait for me, don't go yet! I have to pee!" The clinician yells back: "I am here, I am waiting!" Reesa comes back from the bathroom and says: "Wait, I have to give you a sticker." She gives the clinician a sticker of a dinosaur, and then says: "I will give five more stickers." The clinician says: "How come I get so many stickers?" Reesa says: "Because you did a good job."

2. **When the child is having a difficult time at the end of the session (crying, complaining, or being angry), the clinician speaks about the difficulty of saying good-bye and makes available a symbolic transitional object, such as a sticker or a drawing made during the session, as a tangible reminder of the clinician.**

Example: Sandy, age 2, cries bitterly when the clinician gets ready to leave the home at the end of the session. She follows the clinician into the front yard and clutches her skirt to hold her back. The clinician kneels down, looks closely at Sandy, and says: "It is hard to say good-bye. You want me to stay and play with you and your mommy. Let's look for something that will make you feel better." She asks the mother for help, and together they find a colorful pebble lying on the grass. Very ceremoniously, the clinician puts the pebble in Sandy's hand and says: "This pebble will be with you until I come back." She repeats this twice as Sandy looks closely, first at the pebble and then at the clinician. She stops crying and is able to wave good-bye with her mother's help.

3. **When the child shows distress at the clinician's impending departure, the clinician plays a game of peek-a-boo or hide-and-seek to help the child learn that reunion follows a separation, involving the parent whenever possible.**

> *Example:* Amelia, 15 months, throws herself on the floor and flails while screaming when the clinician says it is time to say good-bye. The clinician says, with much drama: "I have an idea for a game! Can you find me if I hide?" She crouches behind a chair, in plain view, and Amelia, with tears still streaming down her face but a smile on her face, goes to find her. The clinician then asks if Amelia can hide. Amelia hides, and the clinician finds her. They play in this way for a few minutes, and then the clinician asks the mother if she can continue this game. The mother agrees, and the clinician says to Amelia: "Your mommy will do it now, because I have to go." Amelia gets very serious, but she quickly turns to her mother to continue the game, and the clinician says a quick good-bye as she leaves.

4. **When the child shows anger without linking it to the separation, the clinician makes this link by interpreting the child's behavior and reassures the child.**

> *Example:* Khalil, age 4, throws a small toy car at the clinician when it is time to end the session. The clinician says: "You are telling me that you are angry at me for leaving. We were having such a good time playing that it is hard to stop. I will think about you when I am away, and I promise that we will play again when I come back."

5. **When the child shows distress about the separation, the clinician speaks about the separation and tells the child that they will think of each other until it is time to see each other again.**

> *Example:* Linda, age 4, says: "I want to go with you" when the clinician gets ready to go. The clinician says: "That would be nice. I know you want to come with me because it's nice to be together. You know what, I will think of you when I am away, and you can think about me too and what a good time we had together."

6. **When the child shows anger at the clinician in the weeks preceding the termination of treatment, the clinician makes direct links between the child's anger and the termination.**

   Example: Hillary, age 5, says to the clinician: "I don't like you any more" and throws a toy in her direction when the clinician says it is time to end the session. The clinician says:"You are remembering that soon you and your mom will not be coming to see me anymore. We will miss each other, and it makes you angry that it has to be that way."

7. **When the child shows anger or distress at the clinician in the weeks preceding the termination of treatment, the clinician makes direct links between the child's feelings at termination and the child's feelings about the father's absence.**

   Example: Timothy, age 3, sobs inconsolably when he cannot find a little car that he was playing with. He screams at the therapist: "You lost it!" The therapist says: "Timothy, I am so sorry. Your car is lost, and your daddy is lost, and soon I'll be lost and stop coming to see you." Timothy continues crying, but in a more subdued way. The therapist continues speaking softly, saying: "It is hard when you can't find the things you want. I am sorry." Timothy's mother opens up her arms to him and he cuddles up against her. She says: "I will be with you, Timothy. I will help you."

SECTION III

CASE MANAGEMENT

CASE MANAGEMENT, defined most succinctly as concrete assistance with problems of living, is an integral component of child–parent psychotherapy when working with families facing socioeconomic hardship. This is a natural extension of the model's emphasis on the importance of the ecological/transactional context in supporting child development. Child–parent psychotherapists utilize their intimate knowledge of the family circumstances to identify areas where additional support is needed, to link the family with the appropriate resources, and to monitor the integration of the different services.

The goal of concrete assistance with problems of living is not only to resolve problems in the moment but also to provide a learning opportunity so that parents can learn to solve similar problems on their own. The clinician informs the parent about community resources, models for the parent how to contact these resources, guides the parent in taking the initiative in making use of the resources, and provides feedback on additional steps that might be needed to maximize the usefulness of the services. This model can be used, for instance, to help the parent make appropriate use of medical care, to secure good quality child care, to work out transportation problems, to resolve problems at work, and to improve the quality of housing.

For some families, the concrete needs are so continuous and pervasive that the child–parent psychotherapist cannot at the same time provide mental health intervention and case management without an unrealistic drain on his or her time and energy. In these cases, it is important to connect the family to community resources whose mission is to provide these services.

Some programs have case managers and child–parent psychotherapists performing their services separately within the program. This model is feasible when both service providers have compatible views of what the family needs and when they communicate well with each other about the actions they are taking on behalf of the family. Regular meetings between the service providers are recommended as a way of ensuring that there is a unified plan of action to address the family's needs.

Working with families who are exposed to violence often calls for extensive involvement with Child Protective Services and with the family court system. The following describes the model's approach to involvement with these systems.

When Possible Child Abuse Occurs: Reporting to Child Protective Services

Marital violence tends to overlap with a high incidence of child abuse, which might be perpetrated by either parent whether they are living together or not. The child abuse episode might be witnessed by the clinician in the course of a session, or the child or the parent might describe during the session a past incident that may qualify as child abuse.

This is invariably a very difficult therapeutic situation because, no matter how thoughtfully and competently it is handled, it threatens the viability of the treatment. Even in situations where the perpetrator is not the parent but a third party, the parent might feel burdened and threatened by the intervention of CPS and the legal system. Nevertheless, the clinician cannot refrain from making a child abuse report due to fear that the treatment will be damaged or terminated. Clinicians are legally obligated to report suspected abuse, and the investigation to confirm or disconfirm child abuse is not within their power but is the province of CPS.

Nevertheless, a clinician can and should explore what happened in order to make a useful report. For example, seeing a bruise on a child's forehead is not, by itself, sufficient grounds for a report if the parent and the child provide a clear and cogent explanation that the child bumped her head against a hard surface and there is no reason to suspect otherwise (such as previous reports of similar incidents, a history of abuse, parental neglect, or lack of impulse control toward the child). Conversely, vague and contradictory explanations in the context of other risk factors call for making a report.

When the clinician decides to make a report, every effort should be made to inform the parent before actually making the report. Optimally, the parent should be told privately and in person, even if this means having to speak on the phone or schedule an additional session. It is essential that sufficient time be allotted, so that there is an opportunity to process and bring temporary closure to the strong feelings that will emerge. In order to be constructive and protect the treatment, a report should optimally follow the six steps described here.

1. The clinician explains to the parent that she or he has a legal obligation to report the incident, and stresses that this report in no way implies a lessened commitment to working with the family. It is often helpful to explain that the abuse incident is a sign that the intervention is not helping enough to keep the child safe, and that additional services are needed to make sure this happens.

2. The clinician tells the parent that, although it is not possible to know how CPS will proceed (i.e., whether a case will be opened or not, and what placement decisions will be made), the clinician is willing to meet jointly with the CPS worker and the parent, and to participate collaboratively in drawing up a plan of action that will simultaneously protect the child's safety and support the parent in protecting the child. The clinician also assures the parent that no information will be provided to the CPS worker without first discussing it with the parent, and that information not directly related to the abuse incident will remain confidential unless the parent requests otherwise.

3. The clinician encourages the parent to take the initiative in phoning CPS to make the report during the session, and offers support in helping the parent to do so. If the parent declines to make the call, the clinician offers to make the phone call during the session and in the parent's presence. This enables the parent to hear the clinician's report as it takes place, and increases her confidence in the clinician's good will.

4. After the report is made, the clinician elicits the parent's reactions, including the fear that the child will be placed in foster care. Whenever plausible and consistent with the child's safety, the clinician reassures the parent that she or he will make every effort to

ensure that the child is not removed from the home, including testifying in court if necessary. If foster placement might be indicated, the clinician discusses with the parent the reasons for this possibility, eliciting the parent's reactions. Feelings of anger toward the clinician for making the report are acknowledged and legitimized. A plan is made for keeping in touch over the telephone before the next session, and the date for the following session is scheduled.

5. If the CPS worker requests a written report, the clinician informs the parent, eliciting her input about the content of the report. Before mailing it, the clinician shows the report to the parent, asks for approval, and makes the changes suggested by the parent if appropriate.

6. Throughout the steps outlined above, the clinician keeps in mind what the child's involvement in the reporting process should be and discusses this with the parent. Depending on the child's age and developmental level, a simplified explanation might be necessary to prepare the child for the possibility of an individual interview with the CPS worker. During this explanation, the emphasis should be kept on the wish of the parent and the clinician to make sure that the child is safe, and the need for help to make sure this happens.

Although the six steps are optimal in maximizing the chances that the parent will not be alienated by the referral to CPS, circumstances are often such that an orderly CPS referral cannot be made. Sometimes the report to CPS is made by someone outside the treatment and the parent suspects the clinician. The clinician is then in the awkward position of having to deny her involvement but at the same time probe about the events leading to the referral in order to decide on a plan of action. Other times the parents respond explosively and refuse further contact when the clinician informs them that a CPS report must be made. It can also happen that the CPS intervention is conducted in a way that is deeply offensive to the parents, and in their anger at the child welfare worker the parents also become suspicious and angry with the clinician. In all these circumstances, the clinician must strive to keep personal emotions contained and not over-identify with any of the parties involved. This stance will allow the clinician to play a useful role as a caring but objective broker between the parent and the legal system.

There are cases where the parent is so unpredictable and dangerous that the clinician fears for his or her personal safety in telling the parent that a report will be made. In these circumstances, the clinician must place personal safety above other considerations. This might involve informing the parent over the phone that a report was made, discontinuing home visits, and substituting office visits if appropriate until the situation is considered to be safe.

When Custody Problems Occur: Working With the Family Court System

High-conflict divorce and bitter custody disputes often follow the termination of a marriage or live-in relationship due to domestic violence. One common configuration is that the battered woman fears that unsupervised visitation or overnight visits with the violent father will endanger the child's safety. The father, however, frequently denies that the violence took place or that is was as severe as portrayed by the mother, and argues that his parental rights should not be jeopardized. Charges and countercharges of child endangerment and of parental alienation can lead to protracted legal disputes in which both sides try to muster evidence to support their respective positions.

Child therapists are often placed at the center of these legal disputes because of their intimate knowledge of the child's emotional experience. Child–parent psychotherapists are in a particularly difficult situation because they have knowledge not only of the child's functioning, but also of the emotional status of the parent with whom they work. As a result, that parent may ask the therapist to provide testimony about his or her adequacy as a parent or about the impact of domestic violence on the child. The other parent may seek access to clinical material to support his or her position to the court.

There are no simple solutions to the clinical dilemmas posed by complex legal situations. However, there are some working principles that may guide the therapist's thinking in deciding on a course of action that will protect the therapeutic process from becoming a prey to legal disputes. These principles are listed here. To make the use of gender-linked pronouns easier to follow, these principles are written as if the mother is the battered parent and seeking child–parent psychotherapy, and the father is the violent parent. Clearly, the principles apply also if the situation is reversed.

1. At the beginning of treatment, clarify with the participating parent whether the other parent (e.g., the father) has legal custody of the child and maintains regular contact with the child. If he does, ask whether the father knows about the planned treatment and approves of it. If he does not know, encourage the mother to notify him of her decision to seek treatment for the child. The knowledge and support for treatment of both parents gives the child the clear message that both parents are important and participate jointly in making decisions on the child's behalf. If the father opposes the treatment, explain to the mother that treatment cannot be provided without the consent of a parent who has legal custody. If the mother desires to keep the treatment secret from the parent, explain to the mother that this plan is not workable because it would place an emotional burden on the child by having to keep secrets from the father. The mother can be advised that in some situations the court orders treatment for the child in spite of a parent's opposition, and that this is a possibility that can be pursued in consultation with the mother's attorney.

2. At the beginning of treatment, explain to the mother that the therapist will not provide information to the attorneys for the purpose of supporting petitions to the court regarding custody or visitation. The only information that will be provided involves participation in treatment. Explain that divulging therapeutic information can be damaging to the child and the mother for at least three reasons. First, it opens the possibility that the other party will subpoena clinical records and misuse the information. Second, it diverts time and energy from the therapeutic process. Third, it may limit what the mother feels free to tell the therapist for fear that the therapist will form a negative opinion that will contaminate possible court testimony. During this conversation, the therapist should be careful not to make any statements that can give the impression that she or he is taking sides in the parents' dispute over custody and visitation.

3. It is possible that, in the course of treatment, situations will emerge where the therapist needs to provide information to an attorney, a mediator, or a judge that contravene the initial indication to the mother that no such information will be made available. Each one

of these exceptions need to be carefully thought out because it can have important ramifications in setting precedents about the limits of confidentiality and about what the attorneys and the court expect from the therapist.

4. Therapists must make a clear differentiation between clinical assessment and treatment and forensic evaluation. The lines between the clinical activities and the forensic activities should not be blurred. Confidentiality and improvement in mental health functioning are the hallmarks of clinical assessment and treatment. Forensic evaluations have the goal of providing information to the court for the purposes of decision making, and these are not covered by confidentiality constraints. A clinical assessment should not become a forensic tool for the sake of convenience or for financial reasons.

5. Therapists must remember that it contravenes ethical standards to make clinical recommendations about child custody or visitation schedules without first conducting an objective assessment of all the parties involved and without prejudging what is in the best interests of the child. By the very nature of the therapeutic alliance, a therapist cannot be a neutral, objective party. The therapist's views and opinions are influenced by the nature and content of the clinical process. If the therapist decides to provide information to the legal system about this process, the testimony needs to be carefully crafted to clarify the limitations of the sources of information available to the therapist and to describe the implications of these limitations for the conclusions that the therapist is able to make.

SECTION IV

A. ITEMS THAT ARE ESSENTIAL BUT NOT UNIQUE TO CHILD–PARENT PSYCHOTHERAPY

ALL MENTAL HEALTH INTERVENTIONS SHARE some basic principles that are essential to their effectiveness. One principle is the reliance on a predictable and reliable schedule of meetings that are focused on the client's experience. Another principle is the use of emotional support, warmth, and empathy as essential adjuncts to therapeutic intervention.

Other principles are shared across some approaches but not others. Child–parent psychotherapy and psychodynamic psychotherapies share the view that mental health disturbances can be an expression of internal conflict, and that internal conflict may originate in early experience. In common with intervention approaches based on attachment theory, child–parent psychotherapy seeks to promote secure attachments by stressing the importance of security and protection in the child–parent relationship and by encouraging parental sensitive responsiveness to the child's emotional experience and signals of need. It shares with developmental approaches the use of developmental guidance and parenting education to increase parental knowledge of age-appropriate behaviors and child-rearing strategies. Social learning theory and cognitive–behavioral theory contribute intervention strategies that emphasize practicing new forms of behaving and thinking to overcome maladaptive patterns of functioning. Elements of trauma-related intervention are incorporated to promote modulation of affective arousal and to foster realistic responses to threat and danger. Items that child–parent psychotherapy has in common with other approaches are described as follows.

Items Geared to Building a Safe and Supportive Therapeutic Frame and Daily Environment

1. The clinician is punctual and reliable in attending the sessions.

2. The clinician makes sure that the sessions take place in a safe place.

3. The clinician receives regular supervision geared to his or her level of experience.

4. Staff members have regularly scheduled meetings to discuss therapeutic issues and to provide mutual consultation and support.

5. The clinician makes statements that convey positive regard for the individual client.

6. The clinician is respectful of the individual's point of view.

7. The clinician shows empathy for the individual's distress.

8. The clinician encourages the parent to make explicit statements of loving commitment to the child.

9. The clinician helps the individual client practice realistic appraisals of whether a situation is dangerous or safe.

10. The clinician promotes a sense of safety by helping the individual differentiate between reexperiencing frightening events and actual danger in the moment.

11. The clinician makes referrals for additional services as needed, including psychotropic medication, individual or group psychotherapy, substance abuse services, and developmental intervention such as speech therapy or occupational therapy.

Items That Focus on Emotion, Cognition, and Action

12. The clinician normalizes the individual's responses to trauma by explaining the universality of the response.

13. The clinician encourages the individual to use words to name feelings.

14. The clinician helps the individual recognize and change self-defeating and destructive thoughts.

15. The clinician helps the individual recognize and find alternatives to behaviors that make others angry.

16. The clinician demonstrates nondestructive ways of coping with anger and sadness.

17. The clinician demonstrates and helps the individual practice ways of managing anxiety, including turning to others for help, exercising, breathing, praying, meditating, or engaging in other spiritual practice or relaxing or pleasurable activities.

18. The clinician helps the individual find a larger meaning in the feelings of the moment by linking the experience with other emotionally relevant events.

19. The clinician helps the individual manage despair and place painful experiences in a larger context by reminding him or her of areas of strength and satisfaction.

20. The clinician promotes an integration of emotional polarities by helping the individual realize that good and bad aspects of a person coexist, and that love and hatred can be felt for the same person.

21. The clinician responds nondefensively and noncritically when the individual expresses negative feelings toward the clinician.

22. The clinician helps the individual find and engage in behaviors that promote a feeling of well-being.

Items That Emphasize Developmental Progress

23. The clinician makes available developmentally appropriate toys, books, and other materials as vehicles for the intervention.

24. The clinician encourages developmentally appropriate play between parent and child.

25. The clinician encourages the parent to use books, toys, pleasurable activities, and games to provide developmentally appropriate experiences to the child.

26. The clinician provides the parent with information about the developmental meaning of the child's behavior.

27. The clinician encourages the individual to persevere in efforts to achieve developmentally appropriate milestones.

B. ITEMS THAT ARE INCOMPATIBLE WITH CHILD–PARENT PSYCHOTHERAPY

The forms of intervention that are incompatible with child–parent psychotherapy have in common the use of techniques that allow the clinician to control what will happen during the session. These techniques do not foster reciprocity in relationships because they do not model it in the therapeutic relationship between parent and therapist or child and therapist. Examples of incompatible strategies are given below.

1. Use of "bug in the ear" approaches to guide the parent's behavior toward the child.

2. Use of "bug in the ear" approaches to guide the therapist's interventions.

3. "Flooding" interventions in which the individuals are encouraged to immerse themselves in the traumatic experience.

4. Desensitization techniques in which the individuals are systematically exposed to reminders of the traumatic experience.

5. Curriculum-driven didactic instruction.

6. Using aversive stimuli to change behavior.

7. Didactic instruction that is not based on age-appropriate developmental principles or that is not responsive to the child's individual characteristics or subjective experience of the moment.

REFERENCES

Ainsworth, M. D. (1969). Object relations, dependency, and attachment: A theoretical review of the infant-mother relationship. *Child Development, 40*(4), 969–1025.

Ainsworth, M. S., Blehar, M., Waters, E., & Wall, S. (1978). *Patterns of attachment: A psychological study of the strange situation.* Hillsdale, NJ: Lawrence Erlbaum Associates.

American Psychiatric Association (1994). *Diagnostic and statistical manual of mental disorders* (4th ed): Washington, DC: Author.

Bateson, G. (1972). Pathologies of epistemology. In W. P. Lebra (Ed.), (1972). *Transcultural research in mental health. Oxford, England: U. Hawaii Press.* Oxford, England: U. Hawaii Press.

Benedek, T. (1959). Parenthood as a developmental phase: A contribution to the libido theory. *Journal of the American Psychoanalytic Association,* 389–417.

Benjamin, J. (1988). *The bonds of love: Psychoanalysis, feminism and the problem of domination*: New York: Pantheon.

Bowlby, J. (1969/1982). *Attachment and loss: Vol. 1, Attachment* (2d Ed). New York: Basic Books.

Bowlby, J. (1973). *Attachment and loss, Vol. 2, Separation.* New York: Basic Books.

Bowlby, J. (1980). *Attachment and loss, Vol. 3, Loss, sadness and depression.* New York: Basic Books.

Bronfenbrenner, U. (1979). Contexts of child rearing: Problems and prospects. *American Psychologist, 34*(10), 844–850.

Cannon, W. B. (1932). *Effects of strong emotions.* Oxford, England: University of Chicago Press.

Chess, S., & Thomas, A. (1984). *Origins and evolution of behavior disorders: From infancy to early adult life.* Cambridge, MA: Harvard University Press.

Cicchetti, D., & Lynch, M. (1993). Toward an ecological/transactional model of community violence and child maltreatment: Consequences for children's development. *Psychiatry, 56,* 96–118.

Davidson, T. (1978). *Conjugal crime: Understanding and changing the wife beating pattern.* New York: Hawthorne.

Drell, M., Siegel, C., & Gaensbauer, T. (1993). Posttraumatic stress disorders. In C. Zeanah (Ed.), *Handbook of infant mental health* (pp. 291–304). New York: Guilford Press.

Erikson, E. H. (1964). *Childhood and society* (2nd ed.). Oxford, England: W. W. Norton.

Eth, S. E., & Pynoos, R. S. (1985). *Post-traumatic stress disorder in children.* Washington, DC: American Psychiatric Association Press.

Fairbairn, W. R. D. (1954). *An object relations theory of personality.* New York: Basic Books.

Fantuzzo, J. W., Brouch, R., Beriama, A., & Atkins, M. (1997). Domestic violence and children: Prevalence and risk in five major U. S. cities. *Journal of the American Academy of Child and Adolescent Psychiatry, 36,* 116–122.

Fonagy, P., Gergely, G., Jurist, E. L., & Target, M. (2002). *Affect Regulation, Mentalization, and the Development of the Self.* New York: Other Press.

Fraiberg, S. H. (1959). The magic years: Understanding and handling the problems of early childhood. Oxford, England: Charles Scribners' Sons.

Fraiberg, S. (1980). *Clinical studies in infant mental health.* New York: Basic Books.

Fraiberg, S. H., Adelson, E. & Shapiro, V. (1975). Ghosts in the nursery: A psychoanalytic approach to the problems of impaired infant-mother relationships. *Journal of the American Academy of Child Psychiatry, 14,* 387–422.

Freud, A. (1936/1966). *The ego and the mechanisms of defenses.* Connecticut: International Universities Press, Inc.

Freud, S. (1923/1966). The ego and the id. In J. Strachey (Ed. And Trans.), *The standard edition of the complete psychological works of Sigmund Freud.* London: Hogarth Press, 19:12–66.

Gaensbauer, T. J. (1994). Therapeutic work with a traumatized toddler. *The Psychoanalytic Study of the Child, 49,* 412–433.

Gaensbauer, T. J. (1995). Trauma in the preverbal period: Symptoms, memories, and developmental impact. *The Psychoanalytic Study of the Child, 50,* 122–149.

Henggeler, S. W., Schoenwald, S. K., Borduin, C. M., Rowland, M. D., & Cunningham, P.B. (1998). *Multisystemic treatment of antisocial behavior in children and adolescents.* New York: Guilford Press.

Herman, J. L. (1992). Complex PTSD: A syndrome of survivors of prolonged and repeated trauma. *Journal of Traumatic Stress, 5,* 377–391.

Horowitz, F. D., & O'Brien, M. (1986). Gifted and talented children: State of knowledge and directions for research. *American Psychologist. Special Issue: Psychological science and education, 41,* 1147–1152.

Kagan, J. (1981). The second year: *The emergence of self-awareness.* Cambridge: Harvard University Press.

Kalmus, D. (1984). The intergenerational transmission of marital aggression. *Journal of Marriage and the Family, 46,* 11–19.

Kernberg, O. (1976). *Object relations theory and clinical psychoanalysis.* New York: Aronson.

Klein, M. (1932). *The psycho-analysis of children.* New York: W. W. Norton.

Lieberman, A. F. (1991). Attachment theory and infant–parent psychotherapy: Some conceptual, clinical, and research considerations. In D. Cicchetti & S. Toth (Eds.), *Rochester Symposium on Developmental Psychopathology, Vol. 3: Models and Integrations* (pp. 262–287). Rochester, NY: University of Rochester Press.

Lieberman, A. F. (1993). *The emotional life of the toddler.* New York: The Free Press.

Lieberman, A. F. (1999). Negative maternal attributions: Effects on toddlers' sense of self. *Psychoanalytic Inquiry, 19,* 737–756.

Lieberman, A. F. (2004). Child–parent psychotherapy: A relationship-based approach to the treatment of mental health disorders in infancy and early childhood. In A. J. Sameroff, S. C. McDonough, & K. L. Rosenblum (Eds.), *Treating parent-infant relationship problems,* (pp. 97–122). New York: The Guilford Press.

Lieberman, A. F., Padron, E., Van Horn, P., & Harris, W. (2004). Angels in the nursery: Intergenerational transmission of beneficial parental influences. Unpublished manuscript.

Lieberman, A. F. & Pawl, J. H. (1993). Infant–parent psychotherapy. In Zeanah, C. (Ed.), *Handbook of infant mental health* (pp. 427–442). New York: The Guilford Press.

Lieberman, A. F., Silverman, R., & Pawl, J. H. (2000). Infant–parent psychotherapy: Core concepts and current approaches, *Handbook of infant mental health* (2nd Ed.), (pp. 472–484). New York: Guilford Press.

Lieberman, A. F. & Van Horn, P. (1998). Attachment, trauma, and domestic violence: Implications for child custody. In M. K. Pruett, & K. D. Kline-Pruett (Eds.), *Child and Adolescent Psychiatric Clinics of North America, 7,* 423–443.

Lieberman, A. F. & Zeanah, C. H. (1995). Disorders of attachment in infancy. In K. Minde (Ed.), *Infant Psychiatry. Child and Adolescent Psychiatric Clinics of America, 4,* 579–588.

Luborsky, L. (1984). *Principals of psychoanalytic psychotherapy.* New York: Basic Books.

Mahler, M., Pine, F. & Bergman, A. (1975). *The psychological birth of the human infant.* New York: Basic Books.

Main, M. & Hesse, E. (1990). Parents' unresolved traumatic experiences are related to infant disorganized attachment status: Is frightened and/or frightening parental behavior the linking mechanism? In M. T. Greenberg, D. Cicchetti, & M. Cummings (Eds.), *Attachment in the preschool years: Theory, research and intervention (161–182).* Chicago: University of Chicago Press.

Marans, S. & Adelman, A. (1997). Experiencing violence in a developmental context. In J. D. Osofsky (Ed.), *Children in a violent society* (pp. 202–223). New York: Guilford Press.

Margolin, G. (1998). Effects of domestic violence on children. In P. K. Trickett & C. J. Schellenbach (Eds.), *Violence against children in the family and the community* (pp. 57–102). Washington, DC: American Psychological Association.

Marmar, C., Foy, D., Kagan, B., & Pynoos, R. (1993). An integrated approach for treating posttraumatic stress. In J. M. Oldham, MBR, & A. Talman (Eds.), *American Psychiatry Press Review of Psychiatry,* 12. Washington, DC: American Psychiatric Press.

Olds, D. L. & Kitzman, H. (1993). Review of research on home visiting for pregnant women and parents of young children. *The Future of Children: Home Visiting,* 3(3), 53–92.

Osofsky, J. D. (1995). The effects of exposure to violence on young children. *American Psychologist,* 50, 782-788.

Osofsky, J. D. (Ed.) (2004). *Young children and trauma: Intervention and treatment.* New York: Guilford Press.

Osofsky, J. D., & Scheeringa, M. S. (1997). Community and domestic violence exposure: Effects on development and psychopathology. In D. Cicchetti & S. L. Toth (Eds.), *Rochester symposium on developmental psychopathology: Vol. 8, developmental perspectives on trauma: Theory, research, and intervention* (pp. 155–187). Rochester: University of Rochester Press.

Parson, E. R. (1995). Post-traumatic stress and coping in an inner-city child: Traumatogenic witnessing of interparental violence and murder. *The Psychoanalytic Study of the Child,* 50, 252–271.

Patterson, G. R. (1982). *Coercive family process.* Eugene, OR: Castalia.

Peled, E. (2000). Parenting by men who abuse women: Issues and dilemmas. *British Journal of Social Work, 30,* 25–36.

Piaget, J. (1959). The method of relations in the psychology of perception/Die relationale Methode in der Psychologie der Wahrnehmung. *Zeitschrift fuer Experimentelle und Angewandte Psychologie, 6,* 77–94.

Pruett, K. D. (1979). Home treatment for two infants who witnessed their mother's murder. *Journal of the American Academy of Child and Adolescent Psychiatry, 18,* 647-657.

Pynoos, R. S. (1990). Posttraumatic stress disorder in children and adolescents. In G. A. C. B. D. Garfinkel, & E. B. Weller (Ed.), *Psychiatric Disorders in Children and Adolescents.* Philadelphia: W.B. Saunders.

Pynoos, R. S. (1993). Traumatic stress and developmental psychopathology in children and adolescents. In J. M. Oldham, M. B. Riba, & A. Tasman (Eds.), *American Psychiatric Press Review of Psychiatry,* Vol. 12, (pp. 205–238).

Pynoos, R. S. & Eth, S. (Eds.). (1985). *Post-traumatic stress disorder in children.* Washington, DC: American Psychiatric Association Press.

Pynoos, R. S. & Nader, K. (1988). Children who witness the sexual assaults of their mothers. *Journal of the American Academy of Child And Adolescent Psychiatry, 27,* 567–572.

Pynoos, R. S., Steinberg, A. M., & Goenjian, A. (1996). Traumatic stress in childhood and adolescence: Recent developments and current controversies. In B. A. van der Kolk & A. C. McFarlane (Eds.), *Traumatic stress: The effects of overwhelming experience on mind, body, and society* (pp. 331–358). New York: Guilford Press.

Pynoos, R. S., Steinberg, A. M., & Piacentini, J. C. (1999). Developmental psychopathology of childhood traumatic stress and implications for associated anxiety disorders. *Biological Psychiatry, 46,* 1542–1554.

Pynoos, R. S., Steinberg, A. M., & Wraith, R. (1995). A developmental model of childhood traumatic stress. In D. Cicchetti & D. Cohen (Eds.), *Manual of developmental psychopathology: Risk, disorder, and adaptation. Vol. 2.* (pp. 72–95). New York: Wiley.

Reid, J. B., & Eddy, J. M. (1998). The prevention of antisocial behavior: Some considerations in the search for effective interventions. In D. M. Stoff, J. Breiling, & J. D. Maser (Eds.), *Handbook of antisocial behavior* (pp. 343–356). New York: John Wiley and Sons.

Rossman, B. B. R., Hughes, H. M., & Rosenberg, M. S. (2000). *Children and interparental violence: The impact of exposure.* Philadelphia: Brunner/Mazel.

Sameroff, A. & Emde, R. N. (Eds.). (1989). *Relationship disturbances in early childhood: A developmental approach.* New York: Basic Books.

Scheeringa, M. S., & Gaensbauer, T. J. (2000). Posttraumatic stress disorder. In C. H. Zeanah, Jr. (Ed.), *Handbook of infant mental health* (2nd ed.) (pp. 369–381). New York: Guilford Press.

Scheeringa, M. S. & Zeanah, C. H. (1995). Symptom expression and trauma variables in children under 48 months of age. *Infant Mental Health Journal, 16,* 259–270.

Segal, M. (1998a). *Your child at play: One to two years* (2nd ed.). New York: Newmarket Press.

Segal, M. (1998b). *Your child at play: Two to three years* (2nd ed.). New York: Newmarket Press.

Silverman, R. C., & Lieberman, A. F. (1999). Negative maternal attributions, projective identification, and the intergenerational transmission of violent relational patterns. *Psychoanalytic Dialogues, 9,* 161–186.

Shalev, A. Y. (2000). Post-traumatic stress disorder: diagnosis, history and life course. In: D. Nutt, J. R. T. Davidson, J. Zohar (Eds.), *Post-traumatic stress disorder: Diagnosis, management and treatment* (pp. 1–15), London: Martin Dunitz.

Slade, A..(1994). Making meaning and making believe: Their role in the clinical process. In A. Slade & D. Wolf (Eds.), *Children at play: Clinical and developmental approaches to meaning and representation* (pp. 81–110). New York: Oxford University Press.

Slade, A. & Wolf, D. (Ed.). (1994) *Children at play: Clinical and developmental approaches to meaning and representation.* New York: Oxford University Press.

Stern, D. N. (1995). The motherhood constellation: A unified view of parent-infant psychotherapy. New York: Basic Books.

Stern, D. N., Sander, L. W., Nahum, J. P., Harrison, A. M., Lyons-Ruth, K., Morgan, A. C., et al. (1998). Noninterpretative mechanisms in psychoanalytic therapy. The "something more" than interpretation. *International Journal of Psycho-Analysis, 79,* 903–921.

Terr, L. C. (1981). Forbidden games: Post-traumatic child's play. *Journal of the American Academy of Child and Adolescent Psychiatry, 20,* 740–759.

Terr, L. C. (1991). Childhood traumas: An outline and overview. *American Journal of Psychiatry, 148,* 10–20.

Van der Kolk, B. (1987). *Psychological trauma.* Washington, DC: American Psychiatric Press.

Van der Kolk, B. A. (1996). The body keeps score: Approaches to the psychobiology of posttraumatic stress disorder. In B. A. van der Kolk & A. C. McFarlane (Eds.), *Traumatic stress: The effects of overwhelming experience on mind, body, and society* (pp. 214–241). New York: Guilford Press.

Van Ijzendoorn, M. H., & Kroonenberg, P. M. (1988). Cross-cultural patterns of attachment: A meta-analysis of the strange situation. *Child Development, 59*(1), 147–156.

Waltz, J., Addis, M. E., Koerner, K., & Jacobson, N. S. (1993). Testing the integrity of a psychotherapy protocol: Assessment of adherence and competence. *Journal of Consulting & Clinical Psychology, 61,* 620–630.

Webster-Stratton, C. (1996). Early intervention with videotape modeling: Programs for   families of young children with oppositional defiant disorder or conduct disorder. In E. D. Hibbs & P. S. Jensen (Eds.), *Psychosocial treatment research of child and adolescent disorders,* (pp. 435–474). Washington, D.C.: American Psychological Association.

Winnicott, D. W. (1962). *Ego integration in child development.* In the maturational processes and the facilitating environment (pp. 56–63). London: Hogarth Press.

Winnicott, D. W. (1971). *Playing and reality.* Oxford, England: Penguin.

ZERO TO THREE. (Ed.). (1994). *Diagnostic Classification: 0-3 Diagnostic classification of mental health and developmental disorders of infancy and early childhood: 0-3.* Arlington, VA: Author.

ABOUT THE AUTHORS

Alicia F. Lieberman, PhD, is Professor of Psychology, University of California–San Francisco Department of Psychiatry, and Director, Child Trauma Research Project, San Francisco General Hospital. She is the Project Director for the Early Trauma Treatment Network, a program of the SAMHSA-funded National Child Traumatic Stress Network (NCTSN) that has the mission of raising the standard of care and improving access to services for traumatized children and their families. Born in Paraguay, she received her BA degree at the Hebrew University of Jerusalem and PhD from The Johns Hopkins University. She is a member of the Board of Directors of ZERO TO THREE: National Center for Infants, Toddlers and Families, and she is a member of the Professional Advisory Board of the Johnson & Johnson Pediatric Institute. She is the author of *The Emotional Life of the Toddler*, which has been translated to seven languages; co-author with Nancy Compton, Patricia Van Horn, and Chandra Ghosh Ippen of *Losing a Parent to Death in the Early Years*; and editor, with Serena Wieder and Emily Fenichel, of *DC: 0-3 Casebook: A Guide to the Use of ZERO TO THREE's Diagnostic Classification of Mental Health and Developmental Disorders of Infancy and Early Childhood*. As a bilingual, bicultural Latina, Dr. Lieberman has a special interest in cultural issues involving young children and their families.

Patricia Van Horn, JD, PhD, is Assistant Clinical Professor in the Department of Psychiatry at the University of California–San Francisco, and the Director of Training of the UCSF Child Trauma Research Project located at San Francisco General Hospital. Dr. Van Horn received her JD in 1970 from the University of Colorado School of Law, and her PhD in 1996 from the Pacific Graduate School of Psychology. Dr. Van Horn was the lead planner for the San Francisco Safe Start Initiative, and she is a consultant to San Francisco Safe Start in its implementation period. She is also a member of the steering committee of the Youth

Family Violence Court in the San Francisco Unified Family Court. Dr. Van Horn is co-author of *Losing a Parent to Death in the Early Years*, and the principal author of a major review of literature on parenting in the wake of domestic violence contracted by the State of California, Administrative Office of the Courts. She has lectured widely on the subjects of early childhood development and the impact on young children of witnessing domestic violence.

The Child Trauma Research Project is a program of the University of California–San Francisco located at the San Francisco General Hospital. Its mission is to develop innovative intervention models and conduct treatment evaluation research for traumatized infants and young children. It is a site of the SAMHSA-funded National Child Traumatic Stress Network (NCTSN), where it is the lead program for the Early Trauma Treatment Network (ETTN), a collaborative effort devoted to enhancing the quality and quantity of infancy and early childhood trauma services. In addition to the Child Trauma Research Project, the ETTN comprises the Child Witness to Violence Project at Boston Medical Center, the Child Violence Exposure Program at Louisiana State University Medical Center, and the Infant Team at Tulane University Medical Center.